This is a great story, an anthem to Texas, and a how-to guide of sorts for people interested in creating jobs in the tech sector outside of Silicon Valley.

— Some Bigwig

Billion or Bust!

Growing a
Tech Company
in Texas

Lanham Napier

The Braun Collection
Cleveland

Produced and published by Braun Ink as part of the Braun Collection™—executive biographies and memoirs for a business professional, business student, and general audience Additional formats and companion products are available. For further information, see www.braunink.com or contact info@braunink.com.

ISBN: 978-0-692-17488-3

Cover photo courtesy of Bloomberg.
Printed in the United States of America
First printing, February 2019

I dedicate this book to Dacia, Cade, Avery, and Rackers—I love and admire you. I also dedicate it to Richard Yoo, Patrick Condon, and Dirk Elmendorf, who founded the company—all that Rackspace became would never have happened without them—and Graham Weston and Lew Moorman, from whom I learned a lot about business and business relationships.

Contents

PART I

Texas Upstart

CHAPTER I

Rackspace®

The phone rang.

"Lanham!" It was my friend, Quincy Lee, from Houston. "I invested in a company in San Antonio, and you need to check it out."

The company was called Rackspace.com.

"They need a CFO," he said.

Quincy and I had gone to the same high school. He's a smart guy who runs a successful hedge fund. When he laughs, he sounds like a goose honking, which makes *you* laugh. After we hung up, I sat, thinking about whether to interview with Rackspace. I enjoyed working at Silver Ventures, but I had been observing the incredible lights display that was the internet economy in 1999. While I was sweating it out building financial models, wonder kids were landing amazing jobs at companies that a week later were going public. They were *minting* money. I had never seen so much optimism.

The internet mojo was affecting me. Every day, I talked to friends who were executives at companies that were "e-" this and ".com" that, or about whom I read in the newspaper. They were all on the internet bandwagon, and their new companies were raising millions at skyrocketing valuations. As I plugged away as the lone 20-something in Silver Brand's renovated-church offices, internet company founders were indulging in spending orgies and VIP parties. Although I was skeptical of the environment, I also felt envious that everyone seemed to have found a job at which they wore flip flops and jeans, and earned huge stock option packages.

I thought I may as well meet with Graham Weston and Morris Miller at Rackspace.com, early investors in the company. Graham had built a successful real estate business and made a name for himself as an exceptional entrepreneur. We met at The Mexican Manhattan on the banks of the San Antonio River.

He reminds me of Messy Marvin, I thought.

Marvin is a blond kid from the 1980s Hershey's syrup commercials. Graham had little round glasses like Marvin, although Graham seemed much more comfortable in his own skin than his Hershey's doppelgänger. Graham told me about Rackspace, and I liked what I heard. I began due diligence, knowing I had to work to understand the product and industry. It had been years since I had programmed in FORTRAN and BASIC, and my only internet experience was sending email through my America Online (AOL) account. I bought *How the Internet Works* and began reading.

When people began to build websites in the early 1990s, they had to host the sites on their own servers. Nearly every company in North America had a server closet with a few servers networked together on shelves. The servers ran the company's local network, webmail, website, and data storage.

Setting up and maintaining the servers was a pain because they came unplugged, malfunctioned, and regularly needed upgrades. Every office had someone who bought and managed computers, installed software, trained employees on the software, and managed the server closet. Occasionally, the mail server or internet stopped working. "Uh Oh! *Network's down!*" someone called out, and the network manager went down the hall to the closet, pushed buttons, did a reboot, and the network came back up. That was the environment for web servers.

I also met with Richard Yoo, a co-founder of Rackspace.com. He was a Houston native who started the predecessor, Cymitar Network Systems, in the mid-1990s. He brought on Dirk Elmendorf and Patrick Condon as Cymitar co-founders. They initially planned to develop websites, with internet access and web hosting as side shows. When they couldn't find a third-party company to host the servers for the websites they developed, they realized they should focus on website server hosting more than website development. By 1998, they had a business in web hosting. Small business owners were very happy to offload the maintenance and operation of their server closets.

Cymitar changed its name to Rackspace.com, a company that aggregated server closets into organized infrastructure in large data centers and delivered this as a service to small businesses. The service was called "managed web hosting" or "managed hosting." Richard, Dirk, and Pat built the data centers in nondescript buildings where real estate was cheap. These data centers look almost like a grocery store, but instead of aisles of cereal boxes, they have aisles of computers. Along the front of each rack, flashing green, red, yellow, and white lights show how the machines are performing, and power and network cables line the backs and sides. It's a beautiful sight. Data centers are the internet's physical home.

Rackspace.com operated on a Linux platform because Linux was a rapidly growing, open-source operating system for the web, and Richard and Dirk were open-source advocates. As I read and interviewed with Rackspace investors—angels like Jim Bishkin and Fred Hamilton, plus venture investors like Doug Leone at Sequoia Capital and George Still at Norwest Venture Partners—I became interested. Rackspace represented a pioneering wave of web-hosting providers. Other companies in the space were giants like AT&T, IBM, Dell, and Intel. I felt I had to get in on the internet action! If I wanted to create jobs, this was my time.

Rackspace wanted me to join as chief financial officer, and the board wanted me to help take the company public. For an internet startup, Rackspace.com had comparatively good fundamentals. It had gross margins of about 65%—low for a pure software business, about average for a hardware business, and high for a service business. Rackspace combined all three—hardware through the servers it owned and aggregated, software through the code and systems that ran the servers, and services through its groundbreaking Fanatical Support.®

Fanatical Support drew me in. The story goes that David Bryce, the Rackspace.com VP of Customer Care, was meeting with his team one day in 1999. Team members told Bryce they couldn't guarantee customers would never encounter problems, because that wasn't realistic—sometimes power went out, hardware broke, customers or Rackspace.com made mistakes. But Bryce had developed strong ideas about customer support, and when he looked up those ideas in the dictionary to find ways of describing it, he came upon "fanatical": obsessively concerned with something. He described and explained the idea of fanatical support.

"This is going to be our focus from now on," he said.

People jumped on board and refined the ideas that would constitute Fanatical Support. They agreed they could keep customers happy if Rackspace.com could guarantee a 99.999% uptime level and offer a money-back guarantee if the level wasn't hit. From that 1999 meeting on, they started calling the idea of guaranteed uptime and money-back guarantee Fanatical Support.

I loved Fanatical Support, and I liked that Rackspace. com had big growth plans. As CFO, I'd register our intent to go public with the SEC and we'd start our road show soon because we knew the IPO window would shut down sometime—we just weren't prescient enough to know when. I decided that leaving Silver Ventures for Rackspace. com would be the right career move. I saw potential in the company and industry, and hugely wanted to lead an IPO.

I talked with my wife, Dacia.

"I think you should go for it," she said.

With that, I left Silver Ventures and joined Rackspace. com.

CHAPTER 2

Growing Up Texan

Working at a San Antonio company didn't happen by coincidence. I'm a fifth-generation Texan, and I love Texas. My great, great grandfather, Samuel Willis Tucker Lanham, represented Texas in the US House of Representatives for 16 years in the 1880s and '90s. At some point during his time in Congress, Houston became important to the US economy because an Australian set up a wildcat rig outside of Houston: *Gee, wonder if there's any oil around these parts?* Turns out, there was!

The year after the Australian set up the rig, a geyser exploded from it that was so high, people said it was the most powerful oil geyser ever witnessed. The Australian's oil field produced 100,000 barrels per day, more than all other US oil wells combined, and Houston began its transformation from rural outpost to oil town. That's about the time my great-great-grandad ran for governor and won. As the 23rd governor of Texas, Samuel Willis Tucker Lanham is pictured with a shock of white hair, and a thick beard and mustache (which I find curious, since I'm bald).

Many years later, Homer Albert Napier, Jr., settled in Houston, too. Dad went to Austin to study math at the University of Texas at Austin and did well enough that he even conned a couple of honor societies into accepting him. During his senior year, he met Elizabeth Ann Lehman, whose family had moved from Pennsylvania to Texas to work in the oil industry. Elizabeth evidently found Albert charming, and only six weeks after their initial meeting, when Mom was 19 and Dad, 21, they married.

Dad returned to Houston to get a PhD in computer science and then he became a professor of management information systems. He loved the security of being a tenure-track professor. In terms of personality, he combined a tendency to be a practical and occasionally gregarious business person with that of an absentminded professor. His parents had died penniless, which explained his deep need for job security through tenure. Dad considered himself a rugged individualist and political conservative; he was Texan to the core.

Five years after they married, Mom, who was a school teacher, gave birth to me, Albert Lanham Napier, and three years later, to my brother, JB. My family lived in a standard, middle-class, Houston suburb until I was ten when we moved to Hedwig Village, a higher-end suburb for doctors, lawyers, and oil people. My parents stretched their budget to live where there were good schools. To earn extra money, Dad took on consulting projects.

I didn't have my parents' academic tendencies. I struggled to contain myself in school, and found it torturous to sit and listen to teachers all day. But as soon as school ended, I took off. I usually channeled my energy into sports and odd jobs, like managing a paper route and becoming night secretary at our Catholic church, but at other times, my excess energy brought trouble. I stole street signs, egged houses, and those types of things.

"It's just boys being boys!" It turned out, I had attention deficit hyperactivity disorder (ADHD), behavior that in the 1970s and '80s was considered as "boys being boys." No one I knew had ADHD or took medicine for it. Only in the mid-1980s did people begin diagnosing and treating this behavior.

I enjoyed the Texas pastime of hunting, but my ADHD got in the way. I remember one of my first excruciatingly long hunting trips staying in a trailer with my father; his friend Dick Beeler; and Mr. Beeler's son Carl, who was my good buddy. Mr. Beeler was a successful business owner and had a hunting ranch. Our whole house could fit inside the living room of the Beelers' Houston home, and I loved hanging out with them. Their family taught me about business and life.

Every day on the trip, we woke before dawn, donned our camouflage, and went out to our hunting blind for a day of sitting around and focusing as if no one had ADHD.

The first day I sat in the cold. I didn't mind terribly.

The second day wasn't great.

The third day felt horrible.

By the fourth day, I wanted to get into the Jeep and ride home—five hours on long, straight Texas roads.

I stuck to it, though, because I had no choice.

On Day Four, a Remington .243 rifle on my back, I walked mournfully on the trail through brush and trees. My father and I climbed into our hunting blind, and the Beelers climbed into theirs. We sat, silent, waiting for white-tailed deer.

Texas is cold in January, and the ponds were frozen. As I shivered, I realized my hopes for shooting my first deer were turning into disappointment.

"I'm freezing, Dad," I cried. "I wanna leave."

"Hang in there, Lanham," he said. "We have to see this through."

"I'm ready to go home." I was upset.

"Just a little while longer, Lanham."

We repeated this conversation several times during the next 90 minutes. I couldn't feel my hands or feet, and I wanted to jump around to warm up. But then a huge buck stepped out of the brush. I raised my rifle and took aim. My heart was pumping so fast that I had trouble steadying the gun. I was in the grips of "buck fever," when the only things you feel are warmth, sweat, and shakiness, adrenaline coursing through your veins.

I pulled the trigger and hammered the buck in the neck.

He dropped to the ground.

Dad and I counted the tines on the antlers—an eight-point buck!

As we cleaned him, Dad said, "Even when you're cold and things seem hard, you have to push through and you'll get there."

Hunting was a culture and a way of life for us, and I considered Mr. Beeler a mentor. I got to listen to men talk business at night in the hunting trailers and around the fire. Because Mr. Beeler was a successful founder and CEO of a company, the guys around the fire listened to him. The others—like Mr. Millsted, the founder of a waste services company, and Mr. Roberts, a lawyer, who did a lot of cool deals—were successful, too, and had good stories.

This is pretty cool, I thought during those conversations. I looked up to these men. I knew that this was how a person's environment mattered. People who grow up in a family with physics professors talk about physics a lot, and the kids grow up comfortable with physics. I grew up among men who talked business, and I became comfortable with business. Their examples made me want to own and run a business one day.

CHAPTER 3

Data Centers

The Rackspace.com offices were on the fifth floor of an old building at the edge of downtown San Antonio. Drug addicts wandered around aimlessly, and trash littered the streets. We sometimes had to escort bums from the bathrooms. We had bats, too. San Antonio has a lot of bats—a massive concentration lives at Bracken Cave on the city's outskirts—and colonies of bats inhabited our building. They sometimes flew up the elevator shaft and came out into our lobby. The elevators creaked like jalopies and tended to break down, and the view left much to be desired.

Downtown San Antonio consists of a suite of hotels, office buildings, and apartment skyscrapers, plus a close-up view of the Tower of the Americas, the third-tallest observation tower in the world. It is to the San Antonio skyline as the Gateway Arch is to the St. Louis skyline. I sometimes felt bummed out that from our office, we couldn't see Hill Country, a distinctive feature of the central Texas landscape. The undulating Texas hills are a view I could soak up all day.

We ate Class C-minus office space for breakfast, but

the rent was cheap, and our data center kicked ass. I loved walking into the warehouse-like space and hearing the white noise emanating from the fans and air-conditioning, and I got jazzed by the network operations center (NOC), the nerve center where our network engineers basically lived. As if they were running a small manufacturing plant, they monitored network traffic and vital systems, pushed network patches, configured firewalls, built and swapped out network switches, monitored vital signals, responded to messages and alerts, and built and commissioned new servers.

The engineers were smart and worked very hard because they were on the front lines of our Fanatical Support guarantee of 99.999% uptime. They ensured we had redundant infrastructure to keep servers running and accessible in case of an unplanned downtime event or emergency.

We ran engineering in three shifts, seven days per week, and I think the worst situation our engineers dealt with was a cascading failure, when one system failure leads to another, which leads to another, and so on. You have to find the source of the failure and work your way through sometimes hundreds of additional failures caused by the original one. Also, when they were in a hurry, network engineers occasionally "fat-fingered" their commands, entering a line of code with a mistake in it. This could take down the network. When servers go down and customers lose access to their data, it's not a good thing. This happened at Rackspace on only a few occasions, but when it did, it was awful.

CHAPTER 4

Jobs

When I was a sophomore in high school, an oil bust hit Houston like a tsunami. The best comparison I can make is when Hurricane Katrina hit New Orleans years later, in 2006. That's how geographically targeted that economic disaster was for Houston. In 1986, after many boom years for the oil industry, OPEC fell apart for that year. Oil pricing subsequently became speculative and uncontrolled, sliding from $33 to $10 per barrel. The 70% drop battered Houston companies and workers. People lost jobs, house values plummeted, and banks closed.

I watched as my neighborhood went up for sale. Houston suddenly had 200,000 vacant homes. I knew people had hit hard times, but the fear really hit me hard when Dad returned from work one day. He was still teaching at Rice University and consulting on the side for extra income. He walked into our game room.

"I lost most of my consulting clients," he said.

He didn't have a ton of clients, but I couldn't believe he had lost so many.

"No one can afford to keep paying me." He looked fright-ened, and that made me frightened.

After he left the room, I sat on the couch with the TV on and realized, *jobs are really important.*

I'll never forget that sudden understanding that jobs are livelihoods, and livelihoods are lives. My parents rarely talked about the importance of jobs, but with that oil bust and Dad's loss of clients, I suddenly realized that destroying jobs damaged lives, and creating jobs improved lives.

I figured out that when I grew up, I wanted to create jobs in Texas.

Texas

Davy Crockett said, "You may all go to Hell, I will go to Texas." Like Crockett, I really love Texas—the Hill Country, the hunting culture, the long stretches of road, the politics, the hot sun, the steak, the barbecues, the Mexican food, the football, and that awesome Texas twang. Texas has an amazing frontier spirit, a rugged mindset, and the space to have big dreams and make them happen. Plus, people in Texas are nice to each other and get along; we come together to get work (and fun) done. Texas is the tip of the spear for the demographic future of the US, with a growing Hispanic population and lots of Spanish speakers. People are moving to Texas because it rocks. As goes Texas, so goes the US.

CHAPTER 5

Tech Troubles

In March 2000, the NASDAQ reached a record high, driven by dot-com exuberance. Dot-commers had no idea what they were worth, but they knew their worth was rising and they were happy. I remember the word "trillion" being thrown around a lot because the new US economy would expand by a trillion dollars based on the amazingness of the internet. Price-earnings multiples became irrelevant. A lot of internet companies didn't have recurring revenues, which made revenue multiples old school, too. The result was speculation.

Rackspace.com continued to have pretty good fundamentals. Its first quarter, 2000, revenues were $1.4 million, making it a rare breed—subscription-based, recurring revenues. We were projecting phenomenal growth to nearly $12 million by year end, up from $1.7 million in 1999 and $166,000 in in 1998. This wasn't vapor or fake growth—it was real customers paying consistently for our software, services, and hardware.

Problem was, our marketing expense approximately

equaled our revenues. We were spending big to create big growth, reasoning that we could turn marketing expenses, which are largely variable, on and off with ease if things got tough. To me this was a cool combination. Here we were with recurring revenues that were growing rapidly, and variable marketing costs that we could adjust as needed. That happy combination made me think that the internet, changing the world, and rapid expansion were the idyllic combination humankind and capitalism had always awaited. The "network effect," the term used for something that becomes much more valuable as more people use it, was economies of scale on steroids! The network effect that the internet enabled involved math that hadn't yet been fully worked out, but it was creative and big. What wasn't to love?

I didn't know precisely how the network effect was going to change the entirety of the global economy, but I did know that it was creating jobs, and that made me feel like a kid in a candy store. Knowing I had an opportunity to help create thousands of jobs totally motivated me. I also loved working with Lew Moorman, who was vice president of strategy and product development at Rackspace. He had joined around the same time as I had and was very smart. He had gone to top undergrad and law schools and wound up as a strategic advisor to tech companies. He could be prickly because he tended to apply precise logic to decisions, and he didn't always take into account that decision-making also involves less rational human dynamics like how people feel about the decision.

I knew early on that Graham, Lew, and I had a fantastic working partnership and this was an asset that would help center the company for growth. We got along well and respected each other, and all three of us knew there was magic in and power to our partnership that could help Rackspace grow.

However, there was no magic when Rackspace's prospects for survival changed almost overnight. Leading up to the downfall was the fact that in early 2000, all was going very well with new economy and stock market indicators both pretty strong. In fact, on January 10, 2000, AOL, the dial-up internet company and new-economy star, announced it was acquiring Time Warner, the largest media and entertainment company in the world, for $164 billion. AOL had been around for only about 15 years, yet had the capital and clout to acquire Time Warner, an 80-year-old company. *Wired* magazine called this "the symbolic moment when new media eclipsed the old."[1]

I was working with a couple of lawyers to complete our IPO paperwork. We accelerated our work because we knew markets were hot and we needed to make haste. On March 7, 2000, we filed papers to go public. Meanwhile, Dacia was six months pregnant with our first child and working 11-hour days as a radiology resident. She frequently worked the graveyard shift, and I never saw her. We had busy, separate lives, but as a couple, we understood that Rackspace.com had a window of opportunity and needed to raise capital pronto if it was going to be one of the winners and job creators of the internet era.

On March 10, three days after we filed our papers to go public, the tech financial markets began to disintegrate. Even though on that day the NASDAQ composite reached its internet-era pinnacle, people started to figure out that the new economy wasn't all it was cracked up to be. Investors began to realize that they couldn't support unprofitable companies forever, and after years of shoveling money into ideas-turned-companies, angel and venture investors began refusing to put in more capital. The public markets followed suit.

After we filed to go public, one of our web services competitors, Interland, went forward with its IPO. Unfortunately, Interland "broke," meaning its shares closed below the offering price on its first day of trading. Because it was a web services company like us, its failed IPO shut the IPO window for us. Sadly, the window shut not only for web services companies but also for many companies that were spending massively on marketing to achieve the network effect. Investors began to realize that spending wildly to capture eyeballs wasn't always going to put a company in the black.

At Rackspace.com, we didn't want to throw away all the work we had done to prepare for an IPO, so we filed for a delay. But the air continued to stream out of the internet bubble, which eventually burst. By the end of the third quarter of 2000, Rackspace was broke, and my incentive stock options, like the stock options of most people during internet mania, were worth nothing. I withdrew our IPO filing and knew that with no financing in sight, Rackspace.com would soon be bankrupt.

CHAPTER 6

Two Texans

Dacia and I met at Rice University. In the heart of Houston, Rice has about 800 students per class, and strong engineering and biomedical engineering programs. As for me, I loved economics. The Houston oil bust had fascinated me, and I wanted to learn more about it and other cycles like it. If I observed and understood people's behavior in free markets, I'd better understand the oil bust and avoid destroying livelihoods in my own future.

In high school, I had never needed to work too hard to do okay, but just to survive at Rice, I had to learn how to work hard, focus, and apply myself. Smart people surrounded me, and the professors didn't inflate grades. I spent a lot of time in the library of the Jones School, Rice's graduate business school. One of my professors required me to read *Businessweek*, so I read that at the library each week. Ensconced in the library's periodicals section, I started to read *The Harvard Business Review,* which I thought offered actionable insights from credible business researchers and experienced executives. I loved the magazine, economics, and business, and felt motivated to work hard and do well.

The weekend before the start of junior year someone tasked me with driving a load of freshmen to Pirate's Beach in Galveston on the Gulf of Mexico, about an hour from Rice, for an off-campus orientation activity. (I was a student advisor.) We headed to the beach, where hundreds of freshmen were leaping around in the water having fun. My friends and I, hormone-driven males, looked for pretty girls. Among the many women on the beach, I saw a tall blonde. As she emerged from the ocean onto the sand, I almost fell over. I couldn't take my eyes off of her. (The iconic scene from *Dr. No* always comes to mind.)

Holy crap, I thought. *I'm done!*

"Do you see that girl? She's smoking hot," I told my friend, Eric Klineberg.

"Good luck with that one, dude," he said. "You've got no chance."

I saw that as a challenge, psyched myself up, and walked toward her, determined to have a conversation. I don't remember what I said, but I learned her name was Dacia Hammerick, and after about a quarter of a second talking with her, I figured out that she was smart as hell.

"Do you want a ride back to Rice?" I asked.

She accepted, and I devised a plan to ask her out. My plan was to ask my friend, Will Langston, to ride with us because I figured Dacia would not turn me down for a date if I asked her out in front of Will. I had to find a way to have this woman in my life.

I learned that she was born in Guam, had been salutatorian of her high school in Corpus Christi, Texas, and was majoring in biochemistry and art history.

She didn't exactly see fireworks when she first met me on the beach. She later told me that on that one-hour car ride, she decided she sort-of liked me. To this day, her liking me surprised me because back then I thought of myself as a cretin. I liked to hunt deer and sit around the campfire telling stories and drinking beer. I cursed. I didn't wear fancy clothes. I had no idea what colors matched. I was a 100% ADHD Texas redneck, and to add insult to injury, I was not at all creative. I had never studied art or taken up a paintbrush. My idea of beauty extended to Holland & Holland double-barrel shotguns.

Nonetheless, I had goals, and I spent a lot of time trying to earn Dacia's attention and affection. With sufficient time and effort, I succeeded, and a few months after we met, Dacia and I started dating. On one date, we talked about our dreams for the future.

"I want to create jobs," I told her.

We were at Birraporetti's, a cool Italian restaurant then on West Gray Street in Houston. Dacia remembered that comment because she thought it was totally different from the things other guys our age were talking about. Goal-oriented herself, she thought I was admirably earnest about this goal of wanting to create jobs.

Yahoo, I thought. *I may be a cretin, but I'm a cretin with a goal!*

Despite thinking of myself as one of the less refined college guys you'll come across, I did genuinely have that one goal of creating jobs in Texas. Dacia appreciated my admirable, albeit unromantic goal, and we continued dating. I too was impressed—by her ability to combine intelligence and a goal-orientation with a cultured understanding and appreciation of art and things of beauty. By my senior year, I knew I wanted to marry her. I liked—no, I loved—that she worked hard, respected others who worked hard, loved art and artists, wanted a family, and wanted to live in Texas. Also, she was hot.

On June 11, 1994, one year after we graduated from Rice, we tied the knot at the Annunciation Catholic Church in Houston. We held our reception at the Rice Faculty Club in Houston. Marrying Dacia was the best decision of my life.

CHAPTER 7

One Thing

When you're struggling, you become a little more religious. Dacia and I had a son, Cade. I remember standing by his crib, knowing my dream of creating thousands of jobs was about to become a nightmare. Rackspace was broke, and we'd soon need to destroy jobs in a layoff. I recited the Lord's Prayer. I never asked God for miracles—I just prayed.

I started to talk to Cade.

"Look, dude, it's gonna be okay," I said. "I don't know *how* it's going to be okay, but it's gonna be okay." I prayed to God that it would all work out for Rackspace, my family, and the dream I had of creating jobs. But in life and work, things often get harder before they get easier, and prayers aren't always answered in linear fashion.

At Rackspace we knew the IPO was off; we were losing our shirts, financially; and a consultant was trying to help us figure out what to do. I was a voice of doom, the pessimistic CFO telling anyone who'd listen that things were bad, we were about to declare bankruptcy, and we needed to take severe measures to fix the problem. I explained this to our board every time I met with them, people like investors Lisa Ireland, Palmer Moe, and Jim Bishkin; CEO Graham Weston; and others. I wanted to take action quickly to stem the financial bleeding that our projections showed.

I met on a Friday with Lew and other Rackers to figure out a plan to save Rackspace. Our plan had to be simple: starting Monday, every Racker would focus single-mindedly on profit. Period. End of story.

The next day, a Saturday, I sat in my backyard drinking a Shiner Bock and coming up with a name for our plan: Project Profit. The name wasn't the greatest or most creative (Graham excelled in naming things; I didn't), but the message was clear—every Racker needed to drive profits by selling or saving a customer.

My role model in being single minded about something is Curly, the tough cowboy played by Jack Palance in the movie *City Slickers*. Mitch Robbins, the main character, played by Billy Crystal, suffers a midlife crisis, so he goes on a two-week cattle drive with a couple of friends. While riding horseback one day, Curly offers Mitch advice about how to deal with his troubles.

"You know what the secret of life is?" Curly asks Mitch.

"No, what?" replies Mitch.

"This," replies Curly, holding up his index finger.

"Your finger?" asks Mitch.

"One thing. Just one thing. You stick to that and everything else don't mean shit," explains Curly.

"That's great, but what's the one thing?" asks Mitch.

"That's what you've got to figure out," says Curly.

Curly left behind everything to ride his horse and drive

cattle. Being a cowboy was his "one thing." He taught Mitch that all the answers to life are out there waiting—he just needed to figure out that one thing he was passionate about.

Project Profit became our "one thing."

We rolled it out and everyone worked toward it. Lew and I combed through every detail of the Rackspace cost structure and found plenty of places for savings. We had been spending way too much on marketing, and we needed to cut back and focus on landing customers. We didn't need, for instance, to attend trade shows in Portugal and FedEx booths there. We had no market in Portugal.

Project Profit made people think that I knew what I was talking about and ought to be in charge. In December 2000, the board made me president. I was grateful for the battlefield promotion because I didn't deserve it. I was a kid, but there was no one else around, and they chose me. I'll always be grateful they took a chance on me. I'll also always be grateful that when we were transparent with Rackers, sharing information with them and asking them for help, they stepped up.

My first task as president was to lead us through layoffs. Project Profit had helped our cost structure, but it wasn't enough. In January 2001, we had to cut our workforce. Having signed the offer letters for each hire over the prior year, I felt responsible for everyone we let go. I had made the financial and, occasionally, operating decisions that put us in this situation. Rackers had done nothing except work hard.

"For about 30 people in this room, tomorrow will be one of your worst days," I said at an all-hands meeting. I explained how the next day would go so people wouldn't be shocked. Less than 24 hours later, we brought a quarter of our associates into our offices one at a time and let each one know we were terminating his or her employment. I stood by the elevator and gave people hugs as they left. Most Rackers understood we had little choice about the layoffs, but a few were too angry to look at me.

I felt sad to the core and incredibly disappointed in myself, but I had to focus and repair things. I had to try to make something good come out of this. We couldn't assist former Rackers financially, but we tried to help them find jobs. We wrote letters, sent email messages, made calls, and did what we could on behalf of anyone who asked. Although I wasn't privy to the anxiety of those who were no longer at Rackspace, I know that severe anxiety gripped the people who remained—they believed the company was doomed to fold—and they had survivor's guilt, feeling bad for their terminated friends.

Within two months, by March 2001, we hit our Project Profit goal and became profitable. The feel of the place totally changed—we had swagger! But you shouldn't achieve a goal in two months. *Note to self: aim higher!* The goal itself mattered, of course, but what mattered more was having a clear goal. Hitting our one goal unleashed cosmic energy. With operating profitability, employees began to believe Rackspace had a future. We weren't on edge every day. I began talking about a future that lay more than a month out.

Lanham, I thought, *if you reach your goal nine months early, what do you do next?* The only plausible answer was to launch "Project More Profitable!" I never said I had naming creativity. We launched Project More Profitable, focusing ever more on growth and profitability.

I remember reading an article implying that NTT, a

Japanese company, had disclosed the financials of an acquisition, Verio, in its 8-K Form. Verio was the King Kong of web hosting, and Rackspace was a gnat. Our salespeople had gone up against Verio many times competing for new customers. *Holy crap!* I thought as soon as I saw Verio's financials. The 8-K showed it had about $200 million in revenue and $400 million in losses. *They're losing their shirts!*

I ran up to the sales floor and tracked down Khaled Safourri, a smart sales guy whose extremely good looks had earned him the nickname, "Lebanese Brad Pitt." We called him "LBP" for short. He was charismatic and such a big coffee drinker that the local coffee shop named a coffee drink after him.

"Okay, LBP, we're not losing to Verio today," I told him.

"What do you mean?" he asked.

"Whatever it takes, just win any deal against them today. Verio's losing its ass, and it has a parent now who isn't gonna like that. Let's discover where their quitting point is in the negotiations."

I knew that because of Project Profit and Project More Profitable, Rackspace had a little financial cushion, and I wanted to run an experiment to see when Verio would give up. Every company has its quitting point. I believed they'd quit at a price point where we could still make a profit because we were small, nimble, and focused.

"We have to substitute our brains for their checkbooks," I said.

I knew we couldn't outspend our competitors. We had to outthink them by focusing and over-delivering to our customers through Fanatical Support. After a few days of sales calls, LBP discovered where we could win. We figured out that we could beat Verio every time if we retained our focus on sales and commitment to over-delivering.

We attacked the market with this plan, which unleashed confidence in our Sales Department. When a team believes it's going to win, it's great; one win begets another and the success becomes a reinforcing loop. To give resonance to our attack on the market, we installed a bell in our sales area. When Rackers closed new deals, they hung up the phone, pulled the contract off the fax machine, strode down the hall, and pulled the bell rope. New accounts began rolling in, and the bell rang so much that the clanging became a nuisance. We had to change our bell policy, so we rang it only when someone closed a *big* deal. By the end of the spring of 2001, I deemed Project More Profitable a huge success and talked about an upbeat Rackspace future, one in which we were profitable, growing, and autonomous.

This was a great accomplishment by everyone at Rackspace, Inc., which we had renamed. No more Rackspace. com.

CHAPTER 8

Sacrifice

In the early years of our marriage, Dacia and I rarely saw each other. After graduating from Rice in 1993, she went to medical school at the University of Texas Health Science Center in Houston, and I went to work as an analyst at Merrill Lynch in Houston and New York. My job paid well, but I worked about 80 hours per week. Most days I arrived at the office as the sun rose, worked through lunch, took a sunset break to go to the gym, and returned to work. Frequently, a managing director came into the bullpen where I was working late at night and demanded that a piece of work be ready for a meeting the next morning. With this sudden command, my hoped-for midnight departure turned into an all-nighter. The next morning, I typically headed out to the meeting, presentation, laptop, and spreadsheets in hand and wearing the same suit I had worn the day before.

This crap happened all the time. The bosses at Merrill controlled my hourly existence. I crunched numbers and tried to get through the day without screwing up. Although my bosses were extremely demanding, they also were extraordinary business people. They taught me financial skills and the language of business, and I would lay down on the tracks any day for them, men like Rick Gordon, Rob Jones, Chuck Davis, Ira Green, and Chris Mize.

The big picture for me was laying down a stepping stone on my path of creating jobs. I would need a finance and transactions skill set to build, grow, and manage a company. Plus, Dacia was working longer hours than I was, and days often went by when we didn't see each other.

One day she suggested we buy a house, a not unreasonable request.

But, I said, "Dacia, I've got three dollars and you've got two dollars!" In other words: we can't do it. I wanted to settle in Houston, too, but I needed to build up skills before I had any business trying to grow a company. I wanted and needed the freedom to go wherever I needed to go to build those skills. Meanwhile, she wanted to add a dose of order and stability to our world.

I managed to talk her out of buying a house, but her desire for our own place to live kicked me in the butt, ambition-wise. I knew she wanted us to move from a life of chaos toward a life of order. She had deferred her career plans so I could continue a) not knowing what company I wanted to work for and b) not making as much money as I should (considering the hours I worked). Her desire for more stability made a big impression on me.

I figured I better hurry up and reach the point, in terms of my finances and job security, where I was a card-carrying adult (house, mortgage, car, etc.). I accelerated my pursuit of creating jobs by deciding to go to business school to develop skills and contacts. I also felt I needed to get out of Dodge for a little while. As 100% Texan, I had zero understanding of other places. My whole family came from Texas, my wife came from Texas and wanted to settle in Texas, my interests were Texas interests, and my hobbies were Texas hobbies.

I looked at several schools outside of Texas, but my top choice was Harvard Business School. Rick Gordon from Merrill secured a meeting with HBS admissions on my behalf to explain that although I was a total cretin from Texas, I had potential and would create jobs one day. When I received the acceptance letter a few months later, I knew I had Rick to thank.

I left for Boston and lived on campus in Morris Hall, my first time living solo. I couldn't believe how intimidatingly attractive the campus was. About a dozen vast brick Georgian Revival buildings offered every amenity a student could want. It looked like a quaint, very well-to-do New England town.

I sometimes found Bostonians to be cold, but I did respect Beantown's palpably patriotic spirit. In Texas, everyone flies the Texas state flag; in Boston I saw only American flags, and being in a place where national pride superseded state pride made for a cultural immersion experience. I also loved the drama of the changing seasons. I remember driving up to Vermont in autumn and seeing leaves that had turned every shade God created. They were beautiful.

Of the 800 people starting at HBS in 1995, about 799 seemed smarter and more energetic than any other group I had come across. Orientation involved interactions between hyped-up students who had no clue that not everyone was as rich, sociable, and smart as they were. People initially couldn't stop themselves from name dropping, wearing sharp clothes, driving pricey cars, and talking about their vacation homes.

In November, a classmate asked, "Lanham, you want to rent a ski house in Killington?" Killington is a big ski resort in Vermont.

"Sure, that sounds great," I said. Snow falls about once a decade in Houston and melts the second it hits the pavement. I thought a weekend ski trip would be interesting and fun.

When I saw the spreadsheet with the total cost of the rental, including my share of the cost, I couldn't believe how expensive it was. I was way out of my league. I called him. "No way, dude," I said.

I then decided to try to hang out with other married couples, but without Dacia around, I was a third wheel, so I switched strategies and tried to hang out with the single guys. But they had different interests. I remember going to parties at Boston College with single HBS pals and watching them drop the "H-bomb" like it was their job.

BC woman: Where do you go to school?

HBS dude: I go to Harvard Business School.

BC woman: Oh, wow!

I observed the escalations of flirting with mixed emotions—those nights were entertaining, but I felt lonely. I always left early and walked about three miles back to Morris Hall alone. As I walked I told myself I needed to become more extroverted in order to be happy at HBS.

I paid a lot of attention to professors whose classes could help me build a company and create jobs. One had led a big consulting firm and another focused on growing services and tech companies. In class they drew on their corporate experiences. When I went to their office hours to talk one-on-one, professors Jim Cash and Carl Sloane made me feel that I had the smarts and drive to grow a business. Then as soon as I returned to my dorm and tried to complete a problem set or write a cogent essay, I felt inept. That's when it sank in: I was just a schmuck borrowing big bucks to be around smart, successful people.

I loved the case method of teaching that Harvard invented. At HBS, you learn by reading case studies about business situations, talking them out with a small study group, and then attending class to discuss the cases. Professors didn't lecture much. Instead, they asked a series of questions, which is called "cold calling." Students lived in fear of being cold called because if you hadn't read the case and couldn't answer the questions, you were screwed; you got a black mark for the day, and if you received more than a couple of black marks, you failed the course.

At HBS, I learned that you don't have to be the biggest genius in the room to succeed, but you have to work hard and be prepared to give thoughtful answers. I eventually made good friends and figured out how to go out and enjoy myself on weeknights and weekends. But by December of my second year, Dacia and I needed to figure out where we'd go after school ended. Dacia was set to graduate from medical school the same month I'd graduate from HBS, so in May 1997, many doors would open. She'd have her medical degree; I'd have my MBA. Dacia would need to apply for a medical internship then become a resident for a few years before she could be a practicing physician.

At that point, with many years of training in front of her, it was she who wanted to leave Texas. She wanted to take advantage of terrific radiology residency opportunities at medical centers across the country. The problem was, I badly wanted to return to Texas. I had always planned to live and create jobs there, and I wanted to pursue my dreams. I landed a job at Silver Ventures in San Antonio, a few hours west of Houston. At that point, Dacia did something I won't soon forget—she canceled every interview for every residency outside of Texas. She ranked University of Texas Health Science Center in San Antonio as her *only* choice for a residency because that's where I wanted her to be.

She sacrificed. Fortunately, her risk worked out fine, even if the career sacrifice would always remain. On match day, Dacia found out she had matched with UT Health Science Center at San Antonio. We would move to San Antonio.

ANGELS

A corporate location consultant probably wouldn't recommend San Antonio as the place to start a tech company. Its metrics for education and access to talent don't compare to those of big-tech places such as San Francisco or Austin. But people aren't metrics or numbers. Fortunately, neither were our angel investors, who *always* supported our location in San Antonio! They and the co-founders were the heroes of Rackspace and remaining in San Antonio.

CHAPTER 9

Built to Last

In 2001, the founder and CEO of a telecom company called me. Let's call him Randy Holmes and refer to the company he ran as Acme Telecom. Acme offered one-stop shopping for phone and internet, and he had a problem: Acme competed with the Baby Bells. They were big and slow, and they practically owned the web hosting services market.

Randy was a big deal, a 50-something businessman who had co-founded and served as president of a telco before Acme. He sat on slews of corporate boards and testified in front of Congress on telco industry matters. Meanwhile there I was, a 30-year-old who considered Curly from *City Slickers* to be my prophet. To say I was intimidated by Randy is an understatement. *Holy crap*, I thought. *Here comes Randy Holmes. He's the real deal. He's gonna destroy me.*

When I first saw him, he made me think of a silverback gorilla—six feet tall with a mane of shiny, gray hair. He had a bunch of people with him. As they sat down, I noticed that one person on his team had a disability, an apparent birth defect of his hand. As Randy introduced his team members, he said, "This job's so stressful, Chuck over here ate his fingers."

Humor that ridiculed people with disabilities didn't go over well with me. I decided I didn't like Randy, but I appreciated that at least he was straightforward in our meeting. He told me he wanted to buy Rackspace. I told him I didn't know whether we should sell. After Project Profit and Project More Profitable, I didn't know what we wanted to do next. What was I supposed to do after the excitement of helping to hold together the company and rally people to a better future began to fade?

I talked about the Acme situation with our stakeholders, and their answers surprised me. By and large, they thought we should sell Rackspace to Acme. Although I had believed for the previous year that my job as president and CFO had been to make Rackspace strong and growing, I realized through these meetings that I had been naïve—my job had been to pretty up the company for sale.

Knowing that our stakeholders thought I should try to sell Rackspace, I put together a team that negotiated with Acme. For a couple of months, we put a ton of time and energy into the deal. Finally, we landed on terms that included a modest acquisition price and an earnout that would increase the acquisition price if Rackspace performed well. In a healthy market environment, revenue multiples for our industry should have been at least 3x, and if I recall correctly, this deal might have ultimately gotten us there, but with a variety of provisions and caveats.

On September 10, 2001, I went to sleep thinking about the call I had scheduled the next day with Acme. *Tomorrow we'll negotiate the definitive documents for the deal.* I had mixed emotions about selling, but I knew that board members and investors wanted the company sold and I was doing my job for them. The next morning, September 11, 2001, I awoke to watch the TV replay of terrorists flying airplanes into the Pentagon and World Trade Center buildings. Acme canceled our call. The stock market closed for four days. The Dow plummeted 617.78 points, the worst-ever one-day drop, and lost 7% of its value overall. Business investment expenditures stopped.

Acme put the deal on indefinite hold. I thought we'd rekindle it in a few months, but with the terrorist attacks following the dot-com crash, the US and global markets were infected with uncertainty. Through December 2001, investments fell by 13%, and mergers and acquisitions dropped 31%. Acme killed our deal.

I knew deals often fell apart, even on the eve of closing on a deal, so I moved past that frustration. My greater anxiety stemmed from our stakeholders continued desire, even after the failed transaction, to sell Rackspace versus my desire to build it for the long term. For months I had been telling Rackers we were committed to building the company for the long haul because that's what I wanted to do to compensate for the layoffs we had conducted in 2000. But on the side, I had been marketing the company for sale at multiples that were no great shakes.

I decided I wasn't at Rackspace to try to pretty it up for a series of suitors. I was willing to work hard to build a company that would create jobs for a lot of people in Texas, and I firmly believed we could do that.

"I don't want our team to go through the distraction

again of trying to sell the company until its market value reaches healthy levels," I told the board.

I suggested we sell when we could achieve a healthy multiple. I thought our board directors and investors would disagree with my strong point of view on the matter, but they agreed that under the circumstances we should operate under a no-sale board provision. This became a pivot point that enabled Rackspace to think long term. We developed a long-term growth plan, and in late 2002 and early 2003, I laid out where I wanted the company to be in ten years. I shared with Rackers a plan that showed how we'd reach a billion dollars in sales.

Most people believed this path to a billion was nuts. No San Antonio technology company had grown to a billion in revenues. We were in a tech industry Great Depression, and here I was showing charts in which our national dominance and global reach brought us to a billion in revenues. To boot, shortly after that, I had a conversation that might have shaken some CEOs or at least made them think twice about a path to a billion. Remember Interland, the company with the IPO that shut the window on Rackspace's first attempt at an IPO back in 2000? It resurfaced. A guy named Joel Kocher was leading the company. He had been president of worldwide sales, marketing, and services at Dell, and trade pub *Ad Age* called him the "kamikaze marketing guy."[2] He was all brashness and bravado.

I considered him a legend in his own mind, but when he said he wanted to meet with me, I agreed to the meeting. I was curious to know what Interland and Joel wanted from us and figured I could gather good competitive intelligence. Joel and I both knew the elephant in the Rackspace conference room was that Interland had just raised $400 million in capital. The industry knew Interland was feeling flush, and I knew Joel wouldn't be able to hide his glee.

We enjoyed pleasantries, and as the meeting progressed, he couldn't resist being big and bad, as I suspected would be the case.

"You hear that train coming down the track?" he asked. "We've got $400 million, and that train you hear is us coming down the track at you."

He paused for dramatic effect so that I could understand fully the pain and suffering that would be caused when the oncoming Interland train hit Rackspace.

"Either you sell to me or I am gonna crush you," he threatened.

That meeting epitomized Joel, and it stuck in my craw as I created and shared with our team the goal of a billion in sales. Looking back, the goal for a billion was crazy, but I had my mind set and nothing was going to stop me. Lanham Land, a term affectionately coined by Dacia, describes the world I enter in which I expect magical things to happen and be implemented, delivered, and operationalized, not in generations or decades, but relatively soon. I expect greatness as a deliverable in a package on my desk by first thing in the morning.

When I entered Lanham Land, I often received dumbfounded stares from people, bordering on glares, that asked, "Lanham, what world are you living in?"

Lanham Land involves me being optimistic about when and how things will be done, and that optimism involves distortion. (It can become a distorted pessimism as well.) But it's also how I get things done. When I unveiled the plan to hit a billion in sales while we were still at $50 million or $60 million in revenues, most people thought we had officially entered Lanham Land.

But I believed in the plan. I thought that people often tragically overestimated what they could do in one year, and they just as tragically underestimated what they could do in five years. I wanted us to think long term like China. That country of 1.4 billion people does not suffer from a lack of long-term thinking—it plays the 100-year game, and as a consequence, it invests big in a big future. I wanted our strategy in San Antonio to be long term, for us to believe that one of our main competitive advantages was that we made investments for a big, long-term, billion-dollar future. I thought that although we might not have a huge base of knowledge workers, we could think bigger and longer term; our moves today would make us a force to be reckoned with in ten years.

Yes, ten years was an eternity in the tech markets where product lifecycles are about two years. And it was an eternity in venture capital markets where investment horizons are about five years. It also was an eternity in the capital markets, where horizons are quarterly, and in politics, where four-year cycles dominate. But it wasn't an eternity to Rackspace.

In San Antonio, I wanted us and our incredible employees to pursue a strategy that was about being built to last. That's how we would win in the roughly $13 billion global managed hosting market.

CHAPTER 10

Alamo

My bosses' passions were salsa and packaged goods—not my passions—but my passion was learning from the masters, and my bosses at Silver Ventures were definitely masters. One, Rod Sands, had been president of Pace Foods, a family-owned business specializing in Mexican condiments like salsa. San Antonio has a cool role in US gastronomy—it is the place where chili, Cheetos, and Fritos were invented. It was the ideal place for Rod to grow Pace Picante Sauce and for Silver Ventures to be.

Rod had overseen Pace during a time when salsa began to catch up with (and eventually surpass) ketchup as America's most popular condiment. When Campbell Soup Company decided it wanted Pace's Mexican condiment product, Rod managed to sell Pace to Campbell for $1.1 billion. I thought this was an act of value creation worth understanding and trying to emulate. Working with Rod was priceless. He is a leadership guru.

I also worked for Kit Goldsbury, former owner and CEO of Pace. As a creative genius, he had a peculiar way of thinking. He could transform the ordinary into the extraordinary. Take our office space, for example. Kit loved Mexican art, so he transformed a former church into a hacienda-style office space. He decorated it with hand-painted turquoise and terra cotta Spanish tiles, colonial Mexican furniture in the offices, hallway benches covered in traditional serape fabric, and Mexican folk art.

Rod and Kit could teach me what I needed to know to run a business. Sitting at the knees of master business thinkers, I went to meetings that no 28-year-old had a right to attend, and I helped make decisions about acquisitions and divestitures. I was learning how to take the case studies I did at HBS and the number crunching I did at Merrill and produce real-world results.

Dacia and I did enjoy living in San Antonio. I'm one-third redneck, one-third thinker (cerebral), one-third job creator. San Antonio was a place where I could scratch those three itches. The city in the early 2000s was slightly over half the size of Houston and the third-largest city in the state (in 2011, it surpassed Dallas to become the second largest). It's on the banks of the San Antonio River, sunny most days of the year, and the low cost of living attracts a lot of retirees.

Over 60% of San Antonians are of Mexican descent. Spanish and Spanglish are spoken everywhere, and the town has the best Mexican food in the US. Dacia and I loved to go to Chuy's and gorge on the creamy jalapeño dip, which is a saucy masterpiece atop tacos, chips, a taco salad—or all three, which is how I enjoyed it, to the detriment of my physique. We also couldn't get enough of the handmade tortilla chips at Paloma Blanca or the margaritas at Soluna in Alamo Heights.

San Antonio has the River Walk on the San Antonio River, sometimes called the Redneck Riviera, and it has the best event anywhere for rednecks and socialites alike—Fiesta! Every spring San Antonio shuts down for ten days to honor, through drunken revelry and high-end parties, the memory of the heroes of the Alamo and the Battle of San Jacinto. During those ten days, you can drink, go to a ball, drink, go to an oyster bake, drink, attend an arts fair, drink, watch a parade, drink, and join other events.

The parties at Fiesta are intense, and San Antonio puts on a heck of a face for Fiesta week; no one gets any work done. As fun as the public festivities are, the elite social scene is also intense. During Fiesta, debutantes from all around Hill Country have their coming out parties at private clubs, and everyone wants an invitation to those. Dacia and I attended a few, and it's unreal—people spend tens of thousands of dollars for their debutante gowns. I think that's insane, but at the events, I always had an angel-vs.-devil-on-my-shoulders debate.

"This is insane," said the angel on one shoulder, referring to the extravagant spending. "God, this beer tastes good!" said the devil on the other shoulder, demanding that I chill out, smile, and have a great time.

Ostensibly, the Fiesta partying is done to honor the Battle of the Alamo, which is a cool story. In the early 1700s, when San Antonio was an outpost, the Spanish government built the Alamo Mission, a compound that educated Native Americans who had converted to Christianity. In the 1800s, Spain transferred control of the Alamo Mission to Mexico, but in 1835, US colonists in the Mexican province then known as Texas began a rebellion against the Mexican government. As part of the rebellion, the Texan colonists forced out the Mexicans and took over the Alamo. Soon enough, the Mexican army returned in force to regain control. Nearly two thousand Mexican soldiers attacked the Alamo and the Texan colonist soldiers and civilians who were barricaded inside. During a two-week, wintertime siege, Mexican soldiers brutally killed every Texan colonist in the Alamo, soldiers and civilians alike.

Davy Crockett, a frontiersman from Tennessee, was supposedly bayonetted and then shot by Mexican soldiers during the siege. The 100% casualty rate is not cool or worth celebrating, of course; what is celebrated about the Alamo is the heroism of the slain resisters, which inspired tons of Texan colonists to sign up for the Texian Army and create a true military force for Texas, a force that later repaid the loss of life by winning battles. The heroism of the resisters at the Alamo make it an icon of American history and the most popular tourist site in Texas.

CHAPTER 11

Nesting

In 2003, Rackspace surpassed $50 million in revenues; I moved into new offices at the Datapoint Building, a run-down facility that Rackers called Dirty Point; developed more web hosting features; rolled out new products; and expanded by acquiring data centers for bargain-basement prices, buying facilities in San Antonio, Dallas, and Virginia.

I liked doing these data center deals. Before the market bust, I had attended a trade show where I had met a Relera executive. Relera was a Denver-based web hosting company with 11 data centers. A big, tall guy, the Relera executive looked like he did double weightlifting workouts every day. Our conversation at the trade show went something like this:

"Hi, I'm Lanham. I'm from Rackspace."

We shook hands. *Strong grip*, I thought.

"You're from San Antonio, right?" he asked.

"Yes."

"You know, we're opening a facility down there. We're going to crush Rackspace."

That dude could literally crush me, I thought. And figuratively, too—Relera had invested boatloads of capital in its new San Antonio facility, a 10,000 square-foot building with a lot of megawatts. *How can we compete with that?* I thought.

But sure enough, a few years later it turned out Relera had built up too fast. It went out of business and put its San Antonio space up for lease. Paul Froutan and I stayed late at Rackspace to work through the leasing math on a whiteboard. Paul was a boy genius, a 4.0 GPA engineering graduate who wore hula-hoop earrings and drove a souped-up Pontiac as if he were a NASCAR driver.

"Dude, you gotta take those earrings off," I said to him when we went to customer meetings.

After 9/11, the TSA people stopped us every time I traveled with him. Being native Persian, his real name was Pouya. He had a thick, black beard and carried a steel briefcase.

"What the f&*!, bro," I said every time I saw him at the airport. "You wanna get us stopped *every* time we travel? EVERY TIME?"

I got worked up about it because in the post-9/11 days, TSA people stopped guys like Paul all the time.

"As if being Persian isn't enough," I said to him, "You have to pack the electronics into the most suspicious-looking briefcase on the planet."

Paul had moved up the technical ranks at Rackspace to become VP of engineering. The night we found out about the Relera data center, he and I stayed up into the wee hours trying to figure out how we could afford the space and what we'd do with it. Rackspace had low profit margins, and the Relera lease would take up a good portion of our profits.

We're betting almost all our profits on this, I thought.

But considering how much money Relera had put into the building, we considered the asking price dirt cheap. The next day we signed the agreement. I asked for the keys and went into the building.

Dear Lord, please help me not to screw this up, I prayed.

I took down the Relera sign and put it in my office.

Damn, that felt good.

Rackspace's aggressive expansion was on my mind when Dacia said one day, "Lanham, I was pushing Cade in his stroller today, and I saw a home I'd like to buy . . ."

I felt dog-tired, but Dacia pressed on, telling me about a wooded lot two blocks away. Although she would lead the purchase and financing of the house, I still let the stress get the best of me.

"Damn, Dacia, we don't have any money," I said.

I knew this was her decision to make, though. When Cade was born, our financial situation meant she couldn't afford unpaid maternity leave. Dacia's earnings were our main cash flow, and they ensured we'd always eat dinner, even if I lost my job, salary, and stock options. I was Mr. Equity, and she was Mrs. Cash Flow. With me traveling all the time trying to save the business from bankruptcy and Dacia having to return to work, she brought newborn Cade with her each day. He slept in a car seat under her desk.

It was she who pulled in the cash, and it was she who had sacrificed more than I had. I needed to let her be the financial boss in our family. That said, to protect her, I hadn't fully shared with her how tenuous the Rackspace financial position was and how tenuous that made my job. Her wanting to purchase a home meant I'd probably have to share with her the precariousness of my earnings and even my equity stake. I didn't want to have to do that.

Dacia brought me over to see the house and lot, and as we walked around, she developed a vision for the home. I didn't initially appreciate her vision—I thought the house itself was a knocker-downer.

"This whole thing needs to be gutted!" I said.

But I also thought: *Oh wow, this property is awesome!*

"How would we finance this thing, Dacia?" I asked, giving Mrs. Cash Flow the opening she needed. She drove a truck right through the opening I gave her.

"I'll moonlight!" she said, having clearly thought through the financial considerations. She explained that she'd take odd radiology jobs after work and on weekends near San Antonio. Dacia wanted the dream this property represented for her, and she would doubtlessly do what it took to make it a reality for her family.

I realized the decision was really hers to make, and she deserved to make a decision that represented her goals for our family. She was completing a fellowship for an abdominal imaging specialization and would soon be a top specialist in the country. Reaching this point had taken ten years. Every step of the way, she could have done anything and gone anywhere she wanted, but she had always chosen to stay in Texas because that's where I wanted to be.

Buying this property would be an indulgence because neither of us was earning much, and we hadn't yet built up any wealth. We bought the knocker-downer house and lot and moved into it, hoping that someday we'd fulfill our earning potential and have the money to tear down the house and build a new one.

In 1994, Dacia and I married. Marrying Dacia is the best decision I've ever made. She is caring, smart, beautiful, and hard-working, and she let me be the entrepreneur and person I wanted to be. This is in Corpus Christi, on the patio of her parents' house.

After witnessing the fall-out (unemployment) of the 1980s oil bust in Houston, I knew I wanted to create jobs. At Rackspace, I could do that; we grew the company from about 100 employees (when I joined) to nearly 6,000 (when I left). For a healthy America, we need good jobs in every state, beyond tech-meccas. *(Billy Calzada/San Antonio Express-News/ZUMA Wire)*

A data center houses many thousands of servers that generate a lot of heat. When you walk into a data center, you hear the sounds of fans and HVAC working to keep the center cool. I loved the sound of that white noise. (The data center pictured here is not a Rackspace data center.) *(Getty Images)*

AGREEMENT OF LIMITED PARTNERSHIP

OF

RACKSPACE, LTD.

   This Agreement of Limited Partnership (hereinafter referred to as the "Agreement") is entered into the 29th day of December, 1998, between Macroweb, LC, a Texas limited liability company (the "General Partner"), Trout, Ltd, a Texas limited partnership ("Trout"), Richard Yoo ("Yoo"), Patrick Condon ("Condon") and Dirk Elmendorf ("Elmendorf) (Trout, Yoo, Condon and Elmendorf are sometimes referred to herein as the "Limited Partners"). The General Partner and the Limited Partners are sometimes hereinafter collectively referred to as the "Partners."

W I T N E S S E T H:

   WHEREAS, the parties hereto desire to form the Partnership in order to more conveniently conduct all business for which a partnership may be formed:

   Now, THEREFORE, for good and valuable consideration, the receipt and sufficiency of which are hereby acknowledged, the parties hereto agree as follows:

(from Onecle.com)

Richard Yoo (top, in 2007) and his Rackspace co-founders, Dirk Elmendorf and Patrick Condon, went to Trinity University in San Antonio. In the late 1990s, they maxed out a credit card to purchase a server that they could rent out to customers—the beginnings of Rackspace Managed Hosting.

Graham Weston (top) invested very early in Rackspace and was CEO when I joined. He came up with creative, big ideas. Lew Moorman (bottom) led strategy and product development when I joined Rackspace. His brilliance inspired people. Graham, Lew, and I had a dynamic and very productive partnership and, despite our often-differing views (and the fact that, ultimately, our partnership soured), we helped Rackspace achieve big results for a decade. I saw our disagreements as the friction that polishes a diamond. *(Weston photo credit: Kin Man Hui/San Antonio Express-News/ZUMA Wire. Moorman photo credit: © San Antonio Express-News via ZUMA Wire)*

This was Weston Centre, where Rackspace had its first corporate offices and first data center, on the 5th floor.

Rackers who provided outstanding customer service won the Fanatical Jacket Award (a straightjacket). Racker David Bryce coined the term "Fanatical Support" in 1999. Our guaranteed uptime and complete customer satisfaction set Rackspace apart from commodity competitors. Pictured here are various Rackers (including Graham Weston and me) wearing the straightjacket. *(Top left photo in collage by Carlos Javier Sanchez © 2018 San Antonio Business Journal. All rights reserved. Reprinted with permission. Remaining photos courtesy of John Engates.)*

My role model in being single-minded about getting Rackspace to profitability was Curly, the cowboy played by Jack Palance in the movie *City Slickers*. *(Silver Screen Collection / Getty Images)*

John Engates often had to figure out how to make futuristic, unrealistic ideas (mostly mine) a reality. After rolling out our Microsoft-based "Intensive Hosting," product, he became CTO of Rackspace. *(Photo courtesy of John Engates.)*

Top left: Courtney Pena (now Skarda) led our Q-team, which did our lead qualifying. When I became obsessed with differentiating Rackspace through quality phone calls and services delivery, she and her team rose to the challenge. She was a total stud.

Top right: A genius, Paul "Pouya" Froutan moved up the technical ranks to become VP of engineering. *(Photo courtesy of John Engates.)*

Middle: I truly loved Karla Fulton. She had an instinct to care for people, and that was beautiful. She set up the original HR function for Rackspace.

Bottom: Glenn Reinus joined Rackspace in 2003 to become our head of sales. He was entrepreneurial, successful, and a total class act. *(Photo courtesy of John Engates.)*

I loved bringing my son, Cade, and daughter, Avery, to work with me. They were my little buddies. *(Photo courtesy of John Engates.)*

PART II

Growth

CHAPTER 12

Partnership

Graham Weston and I talked every weeknight because our phone conversations helped keep our working relationship strong. We also met weekly for a couple of hours. Talking frequently made us better business partners, and we knew that to stay aligned with each other, we had to put in the time.

I liked that Graham had big ideas; was open minded, creative, and driven; and possessed courageous vision. Although his family heritage involved the British upper crust, he had grown up in San Antonio. After starting a successful photography business in high school, he went to Texas A&M University. He spent his early career in commercial real estate and then invested in and became CEO of Rackspace.

Graham had absolute belief in the company and formed the foundation of the idea that Rackspace was here to stay. His view was that it would be around for a long time, and we would all do good things. One of his biggest contributions to Rackspace was our culture. In 2003, some managers and executives at Rackspace went to a leadership seminar in which people's strengths and weaknesses were determined and a path toward better leadership was developed. Graham didn't agree with how the assessment of his leadership style was done. Dissatisfied, he went out to find an evaluation system that he liked, one he felt could be used for developing our people and culture. He found a system called Strengths-Finder, which helps people identify their strengths and then use them in the workplace. People who use their strengths every day are more likely to be engaged and productive, and less likely to quit their jobs.

Graham loved the StrengthsFinder system and became highly committed to seeing it through as a way for Rackspace to develop a culture based on strengths. He went to a seminar to become a coach for StrengthsFinder, and began using it to figure out how each Racker's strengths could best fit into teams and the company as a whole. He started experimenting with creating teams, trying to fit people's strengths together like Lego pieces.

I was happy Graham wanted to use a system to develop people and a great culture at Rackspace, but he and I could frustrate each other. Most of all, what frustrated me was that working through his ideas, whether good or bad, took up a lot of time and resources that I didn't feel I had. Any idea, no matter how good it is, takes a number of people to implement. The trouble with ideas is they don't come with magic dust to implement them and turn them into profits.

As the guy responsible for leading the company operations, implementing the best ideas, and getting things done well and on time, I spent lots of cycles turning strategic thinking into sustainable growth and profits. I was outcome-oriented, had a sense of urgency, and made sure to mobilize Rackers to deploy new products and achieve goals. Our big picture, the driving idea above and beyond all others, was that Rackspace needed to become one of the world's greatest tech-enabled service companies. If we delivered incredible outcomes to our customers, we could put a dent in the universe. This meant hiring and developing Rackers who worked hard to serve clients in the Fanatical Support way.

While Graham wasn't physically present in the office frequently, Lew Moorman had a mainstay physical (and intellectual) presence. He was super-smart and completely committed to doing great things, believing in the Fanatical Support mission and strategy with every fiber of his being. He was one of the more intense people I've ever known, and he dug into data vigorously, rarely content to rely solely on reports. He liked to generate real insights, and he came up with cool solutions and guideposts for Rackspace based on his insights. I admired his data presentation skills—he could develop exactly the right PowerPoint graph for exactly the right data and strategy consideration. His visualizations of our strategy showed analytical precision and creativity.

With those skills and the articulateness you'd expect of a Stanford law grad, Lew impressed people immediately. He worked a crowd with ease and had a keen awareness of those around him, a natural presence, and a charisma that inspired people. He was more socially intelligent than most people. StrengthsFinder has a trait it calls "Win Others Over" or "WOO." Lew was so good at WOO that Rackers sometimes called him Woo Moorman.

Lew also combined his seriousness and intensity with an ability to have fun. I remember we once held a core values boot camp that had a fun water-dunking booth. He got in there and hammed it up with the best of them, playing off his character as Woo Moorman.

A while into his tenure as senior vice president, Lew wanted me to make him president. I knew that title meant a lot to him, and we'd lose him if I didn't acquiesce. I had the normal concerns you'd have when making a promotion, trying to understand the puts and takes of him in the president role. As smart as he was, he also could be opinionated to the point that he sometimes wore out people's saddles. He loved to debate, and he was a business man who did not gladly suffer fools. I worried that this could dent morale.

All things considered, I knew we'd lose Lew if I didn't promote him to president. I very much wanted to keep Lew's admirable strengths working toward the great, big future of Rackspace. I knew my agreeing to make him president could lead to problems with me because I myself found Lew difficult to manage; I accepted this difficulty as the natural flipside of his intellect and intensity. As soon as a Racker figured out the path to collaborate with Lew, working together was powerful. It was just that discovering the path took some people longer than others. When I promoted Lew to president, my bet was a straightforward one—I believed I'd figure out how to make it all work.

In StrengthsFinder fashion, we constructed teams to fit our strengths together for the betterment of the company and to minimize the effects of our flaws. StrengthsFinder was a good system for doing this, and Graham led it. But what probably helped me more than StrengthsFinder, in managing the dynamic partnership among Graham, Lew, and me, was thinking about the power of partnerships that had a dynamic tension I admired. I needed to understand partnership examples in which the partners couldn't, as the saying goes, polish the diamond without friction. When Lew, Graham, or I had disagreements, I wanted to be able to see the friction as critical toward polishing the diamond.

In looking for examples, I decided I liked the one of Ronald Reagan and Tip O'Neill. They held different world views and policies, and as President and Speaker of the House they fought a lot, but in the end, showed loyalty to the country and accomplished a lot.

"[What] both men deplored more than the other's political philosophy was stalemate," O'Neill's son, Thomas, wrote in an op ed piece in the *New York Times*.[3]

I thought that probably held true for Graham, Lew, and me.

I also admired the partnership of Bill Clinton and Newt Gingrich. In the mid-1990s, they battled over spending cuts, but they respected each other. Gingrich wanted to slash spending and introduce a balanced budget amendment. Clinton wanted to spend money. He vetoed nearly every bill and resolution Gingrich put on the table, which resulted in a budgetary impasse so severe that the government shut down for three weeks. But after that, the men agreed to work together.

"[We] hammered out a really productive relationship," Clinton later said. "We got our work done on time." After they began meeting privately, they realized they could come to terms on many matters. In 1997, they passed the Balanced Budget Act.[4]

These examples of partnerships that had dynamic tension and yet achieved big results showed me that if we put in the effort, we could work through our differences. Thinking about the examples helped me deal with our disagreements. Just as the politicians managed to put country first, I knew we had to put the company first. Assuming we developed differences of opinion over the ensuing years, I knew we wouldn't be the first business growers to have differing views. Thank God, we liked, respected, and needed each other.

CHAPTER 13

Intensive Hosting

Rackspace's cash flow improved on a steady and predict-able basis. After we united behind the idea that we'd have a built-to-last plan and we'd focus on sales, the Rack-space top line grew 50% per year. In 2004, we hit $86.8 million; in 2005, $138.8 million; and in 2006, $224 million. Best of all, our operating cash flow was positive.

By the summer of 2002 and with Fanatical Support as the driver of our growth, we needed to transform our product suite. Bigger customers were contracting with us for web and data hosting, and they often used Microsoft as their software platform. Meanwhile, we had built our software and features and our middleware on a Linux operating system. Our tech team knew Linux was really good and cost less money. But our business team was seeing that the interface between our Linux operating system and our increasingly large custom-ers' Microsoft operating systems could cause problems.

Should we create a new offering that better aligned with Microsoft? That would mean switching from a tech-driven Linux culture to a business-driven Microsoft culture, building our middleware, features, and interfaces in a way that made it very easy for customers on Microsoft systems to use our web and data hosting offerings.

We decided to do an experiment by technologically dipping our toe into the Microsoft pond. We'd develop a Microsoft tech stack and work with some beta customers to see how they liked it. Long story short, our experiment was very successful, and from it, we discovered that when we give customers what they're asking for, they are very happy. The experiment showed us more than anything that we needed to listen to customers and they would always pull us forward, a mantra that became important to our company culture. In large numbers, customers had been telling us we should move to a Windows platform, and with their ecstatic reaction to our experiment, we knew we couldn't ignore them anymore.

We decided to make Microsoft our core infrastructure, moving away from Linux and open-source coding. We would in the future provide proactive managed hosting *exclusively* on the Microsoft platform.

Graham was awesome at naming products, and he came up with the name for our new Microsoft-based division, Intensive Hosting™. But moving full throttle from Linux to Windows and providing enterprise-quality software and services for the Windows environment, including Fanatical Support, wouldn't be easy. In developing our Intensive Hosting offering and rolling it out to the market, we'd face three major challenges.

First, by creating Intensive Hosting, we were entering the business of serving large, enterprise-level clients—a new market segment for us. We had always mainly served small-

and mid-sized businesses that needed to pay for a fraction of a server. Serving enormous, enterprise-level clients made for an enormous change. Second, Intensive Hosting would bring us into head-to-head competition with a new set of competitors who served large, enterprise-level clients. And third, with Intensive Hosting, we'd restrict ourselves to Microsoft as the operating system on our product platform. A sole-sourcing strategy rarely works well because the supplier exerts too much control. In this case, there was a real risk that Microsoft would own our asses.

New customers, big competition, and lack of control over our own destiny are not a promising combination, but not listening to our customers would have been even worse. Here's where one of my few marketable skills could be useful. I'm pretty good, if I do say so myself, at getting people to do things they don't think are possible. I pull them into Lanham Land, the alternate universe in which things happen the way I want them to happen. During the development and rollout of Intensive Hosting, I frequently talked with our CTO, John Engates, about what I wanted in a product. In these conversations, John usually gave me an extremely annoyed, dumbfounded look.

Lanham, what are you talking about? His look spoke volumes. *What world are you living in? We can't do that.*

"Figure out how to do it, John," I usually responded to his glare.

I think John experienced Lanham Land as much as anyone at Rackspace, especially during the development and rollout of Intensive Hosting. He also experienced the fallout of my ADHD all the time.

While discussing unrealistic and outlandish (and also

good) ideas, I pace to try to manage my desire to fidget and look around the room and pull out my non-existent hair. I pace in meetings and when I'm talking on the phone. I do all sorts of things associated with ADHD, like waking up in the middle of the night and sending emails; working intensely, driving everyone nuts, and then suddenly needing to be alone; and experiencing periods when I can't focus on anything and then suddenly can't stop focusing.

If a topic doesn't interest me, I can't concentrate on it. Some days I can't seem to stop my mind from wandering, and other days I catch myself reading about, say, quail hunting, and suddenly realize I've been reading the same quail hunting book for five hours and it's now 3 a.m. ADHD involves lack of focus and then, conversely, acute focus.

When we were rolling out Intensive Hosting, I observed the annoyed, astounded look on Rackers' faces when I asked for very-difficult-to-deliver things, and their looks informed me we were in Lanham Land. But all's well that ends well, and during our rollout, John, a tech superhero, made everything end well! Whenever I asked him to "figure it out," he always did.

John and his team rolled out the seven proactive elements of Intensive Hosting, which included an extremely proactive (fanatical) approach to managed hosting for companies on the Microsoft platform. He led the rollout of Intensive Hosting and its "Proactive-7" elements so phenomenally well that we promoted John from VP of operations to CTO of Rackspace. Under Intensive Hosting and his overall tech leadership, we began to gain the customers we wanted—demanding customers.

A cohort of Rackers didn't want Rackspace to own the

segment of the market known as "demanding customers," but my view was that we should bring it on; demanding customers are usually high margin for whatever company figures out how to serve their needs.

I considered Intensive Hosting a huge success, and almost everyone at Rackspace loved it. We created incredible outcomes for our new, enterprise-level customers, keeping them happy. We started serving large, demanding customers so well that word of mouth and referrals became our primary marketing tools. Within months of rollout, we knew Intensive Hosting™ would continue and extend our financial successes. Sure enough, it became a main component of our 50% annual growth. In 2003, we nearly tripled our number of two-year contracts valued at over $500,000, and we counted ten Fortune 100 companies as customers—companies like The Scotts Company, Motorola, and the NFL, which put their faith in Intensive Hosting. Considering we remained a small San Antonio company, we thought that was pretty good. In 2004, we won the Frost & Sullivan Product of the Year Award for excellence and innovation.

Nerd Bird

A flight between San Francisco and other cities is nicknamed The Nerd Bird. New York has 40 daily Nerd Birds; Seattle, 26; Dallas, 21; Las Vegas, 19; Chicago, 13; London and Austin each have 6; Detroit has 3; and Beijing has 2. San Antonio has one daily Nerd Bird, along with Cleveland, Detroit, Nashville, Milwaukee, Buffalo, and Raleigh, and cities like Columbus, Santa Fe, and Birmingham have none.

San Francisco is the Disney World of job creation and innovation in the US, and if it had more direct flight options from more cities, then working Americans might be more connected to Silicon Valley—we'd begin to build a better web of innovation in the US rather than a geographic world of tech haves and tech have-nots. Subsidizing additional flights to Silicon Valley tops my list for developing better tech ecosystems in the US.

CHAPTER 14

Austin

In April 2006, with Graham as chairman and CEO, Rackspace began to think again about going public. The board of directors thought that as a precursor to an IPO road show, our titles should better reflect our roles. The directors promoted me to CEO and Graham stayed on as Rackspace chairman.

I wanted to upgrade the Rackspace office space. Rackers worked incredibly hard and deserved better working conditions than the Dirty Point offices provided. I thought the possibility of a move necessitated a huge decision—if we were going to take the trouble to relocate, then we should figure out now, not later, whether we should move to Austin.

I had never heard anyone at Rackspace seriously consider moving the company to Austin. Rackspace investors were from San Antonio, and the company's co-founders, Richard, Dirk, and Pat, had all attended Trinity University and met in San Antonio. Just about all the Rackspace employees had grown up in and lived in San Antonio. Rackspace considered itself a dyed-in-the-wool San Antonio company. But as CEO,

I felt I had to consider the possibility of moving. From the standpoint of someone whose job was to execute on growing the company, I thought Austin made for a logical choice as a headquarters location. It offered a much larger base of tech talent, which would improve our odds of successfully going public and growing to a billion in revenues.

If we were going to move to Austin and thereby reduce the risk factors in our growth path, I felt we should do so in 2006 when we weren't yet a public company. Austin is the capital of Texas and is centrally located, about an hour from San Antonio. It's laid back, casual, welcoming, fun, and has a quirky vibe, with an official slogan of "Live Music Capital of the World," and an unofficial slogan of "Keep Austin Weird." Its live music scene has attracted national recognition, as has the massive, annual South by Southwest music and tech festival.

Austin offers a fantastic lifestyle, including 300 days of sunshine per year, great bike paths, nice rivers and lakes, tons of yoga, and a great arts scene. But what interested me most about Austin was its technology strength and abundance of knowledge workers. In 1984, a University of Texas at Austin student, Michael Dell, started a business. He grew Dell Computer into the third-largest PC business in the world. Also, John Mackey, Whole Foods co-founder, began expanding Whole Foods outside Austin in the mid-1980s. In the late 1980s, with Dell and Whole Foods expanding, Austin began to earn a reputation as a business hub.

The tech industry became important enough to Austin that by the 1990s, one of its nicknames was "Silicon Hills," and tech companies were creating satellite offices in the city and suburbs. Today, Dell, Apple, IBM, Samsung NXP,

National Instruments, AT&T, Applied Materials, Amazon, and Accenture all employ people in Austin. Every analysis we did at Rackspace told us San Antonio lacked an adequate pool of tech talent, which would bottleneck our growth. As much as Dacia and I loved San Antonio, I knew that from a business growth perspective, Austin was a compelling location. The education level was fantastic, with about 42% of adults having a bachelor's degree, compared to 30% nationally and 25% in San Antonio. Among other things, Austin has the University of Texas at Austin with 55,000 students.

If we moved to Austin, the plan would be to start a new office and grow it into our headquarters, at the same time moving to a better but not too much larger space in San Antonio. As I was working through the puts and takes of this plan in 2006, Dell began to have trouble. It had to recall millions of batteries manufactured by Sony that it used in its laptops. The SEC launched an investigation into Dell's accounting practices. And after years of high growth, the company started flagging and Michael Dell had to return as CEO. He announced a new strategy for the company, including cutting 8,000 jobs. The layoff became all the talk in central Texas.

Susan Laves, a director in our marketing group, came up with an idea. She was very smart, had grown up in Texarkana, and spoke with the thickest southern twang you've ever heard. Having previously worked at Dell, she knew morale was low.

"Lanham," she asked, "What do you think about the idea of recruiting some talent from Dell to Rackspace?"

"I don't think so," I said. "Not enough of them will be willing to move to San Antonio." But . . . let's see here . . .

maybe we could make something work. I told her, confidentially, that I was trying to figure out whether we would develop our new headquarters in Austin.

"Well, Lanham, let's just instead create an Austin satellite office!" she responded.

She wanted access to the talented Dell people as much as I did, but in our hearts, we both wanted Rackspace headquarters to remain in San Antonio. Susan and I, plus salesperson Glenn Reinus, batted ideas around on how we could gain the benefits of Austin without moving Rackspace headquarters there. We developed a detailed action plan for tapping into Austin's UT graduates and the former Dell people. It started with our quickly creating a satellite office in Austin and recruiting people to it, but we would keep our headquarters in San Antonio.

To believe in this, we had to set a vision in which Rackspace would become to San Antonio what Dell was to Austin. Dell had helped propel Austin into a town that could attract knowledge workers in droves. Microsoft had done the same in Seattle, creating the environment that later spawned Amazon. By maintaining headquarters in San Antonio, we wouldn't have to compete for talent with other tech companies because there were so few. Rackspace remained the largest and fastest-growing investor-backed tech company in San Antonio, so we were, if not the only game in town, certainly one of very few games in town. We could enjoy the advantages of low employee turnover as well as lower cost of living. Our superior cost position would benefit Rackspace customers, and we could supplement where needed through additional talent in Austin.

During the first year of our San-Antonio-headquarters-

Austin-satellite-office strategy, we snagged several former Dell people, including a new Rackspace CFO, a new leader of our cloud computing division, and a founder of what soon became known as our lead qualifying team, or Q-Team. I've always said that if you put aside your heart, you can easily argue that a more logical plan would have been to make Austin our headquarters and San Antonio a satellite office. But our co-founders, investors, and board members were such strong adherents to the San Antonio idea that developing a purely logical plan to move our headquarters may never have succeeded. Our San-Antonio-or-bust plan made the most sense in the real world. When we decided, with excitement and a sense of adventure, that we should become to San Antonio what Dell had become to Austin, this became part of our built-to-last philosophy.

The Castle

We turned our attention to finding new office space in San Antonio. The problem for me, as the operating person in charge, was threefold. First, growing companies burn through space fast. Second, office space matters to tech companies. Third, space is a clunky asset because no matter how you design it, it's never going to be exactly right. If you design a lot of walls, it's too quiet and hinders employee interaction. If you have no walls, it's noisy and employees aren't productive. The way companies construct office space affects how employees perform.

I know that tech company working space *appears* to the uninitiated to be over-the-top, but I'm a huge advocate of the creative designs of tech office space because the creativity serves a strategic purpose. Space impacts how companies operate; it impacts culture and people. In particular, great office space shows respect for employees. Employees toiling away at a computer all day have to have reasons and ways to extract themselves from their chairs, move around, and interact with other human beings. It's a mental and medical fact that workers in the knowledge economy—people who sit at computers about ten hours per day—need creative ways of engaging with one another and with the world beyond the screen. Sitting in a chair for work all day carries more mental and physical health risks than smoking.

I knew we could keep healthcare costs lower by designing office space that helped prevent vision problems and back issues, and reduced frequency of carpal tunnel syndrome and other repetitive stress injuries. We wanted people to work hard but also have fun and avoid burnout. Burnout increases employee turnover rates, and when your assets walk out the door, burnout that leads to high turnover becomes a ferocious problem.

We needed the Rackspace office space to reduce health care costs, honor employees, and enhance employee loyalty. Fortunately, we also could enjoy the fact that by deciding to remain in San Antonio, we could be luxurious about using space to honor our awesome team. We hired Randy Smith, a bald dude like me, as our vice president of real estate. He did a bang-up job touring potential locations looking at all the options for Rackspace. He had been a real estate attorney and was the nicest guy you'll ever meet. He exuded warmth and knew his industry very well.

Graham and Randy worked well together. They were reviewing Rackspace real estate options when officials from Windcrest pitched them on an idea. Windcrest is a suburb ten minutes northeast of San Antonio and technically considered part of the San Antonio Metropolitan Statistical Area. It's basically a city subdivision landlocked by San Antonio that for the most part uses San Antonio schools. Its population is about 5,000. The officials pitched Graham and Randy on converting Windcrest's shut-down, dilapidated Windsor Park Mall into the new Rackspace headquarters.

This was by all accounts a crazy idea. Windsor Park Mall opened in 1976 as a shopping plaza with stores including The Athlete's Foot, Casual Corner, Walden Books, and J.C. Penney, and a food court that included Chick-Fil-A, Dairy Queen, and a game room. The mall stayed vibrant into the 1980s, but then it became a mess. Gangs started to overrun Windcrest, and shootings near the mall became a regular occurrence. People didn't want to shop there anymore, and in 2005, it shut down.

A lot of people would have laughed at the idea of making the former mall our headquarters purely on the face of it and not indulged the idea. When I first heard about it from Randy and Graham, I thought they were nuts. A lot of Rackers had worked at Foot Locker in that mall in the 1980s and 1990s, and they didn't want to go away to school, get degrees, and come back only to work at the mall again.

But Graham almost always embraced the unorthodox and creative. His instinct much of the time was, "Okay, let's do it!" He loved this idea from the start. He was a real estate investor in addition to his role at Rackspace, and he had been working on a theory that malls across the country would fall apart as retail shopping gave way to online shopping, and a lot of their space could be repurposed as tech campuses.

Rackspace, Graham thought when those Windcrest people approached him, *could be one of the first companies, if not* the *first company, to do this mall repurposing.*

In early August 2007, we entered into a $25-million lease for 67 acres and a 1.2 million-square-foot facility. It would house our new corporate headquarters, including a future data center operation. My job was to make sure we could finance it and to execute on every aspect of it. A long-term lease is debt, and incurring such debt is a risk and challenge that most entrepreneurs don't anticipate (but they should).

We spent over $100 million on renovations. We received $72 million in tax abatements and development grants from the State of Texas and the City of Windcrest. The owner of the vacant mall had paid property taxes to Windcrest each year, and we agreed to make equivalent payments in lieu of those taxes to the local school district. The Rackspace Foundation donated $2.5 million to the community, which went primarily to the schools.

A *New York Times* article in October 2012 called the original vision devised by our team "a grand vision of creating a tech mecca comparable to Austin's so-called Silicon Hills, located 60 miles east of the mall and home to Dell and Hoover's."[5] The people at the City of Windcrest deserve a lot of credit for their vision. They saw a way to do something meaningful with tired real estate, and as a result of their vision, their city's tax base has gone up every year.

Malls connect people to stores, and in our renovated building, we retained that "connecting" theme. We made the offices open, casual, and expansive. Each Racker had a desk, chair and cube—which we ironically called our "power cubes"—and we clustered the cubes into groups. We had a chess board the size of a basketball court where people could stand and play chess as human chess pieces. We had the world's largest word search, with the words spanning a long corridor. We had a slide people could use to get from the second floor offices to the food court area on the first floor. We had billiards and pool tables. We named some conference rooms after breakfast cereals (Wheaties, Cap'n Crunch), TV game shows (*Jeopardy*, *Family Feud*), and former mall stores (Lens Crafters, Gingiss Formal Wear). We used locally sourced stone accents, and had towering ficus trees and a lot of skylights to give the building a light, airy, and natural feeling. And we developed at the front entryway a soaring metallic half-arch, giving the mall entry a towering, modern feel as opposed to a short, squat feel.

The open space facilitated and encouraged the flow of communication. This was tech space for tech workers. We maximized the ability for people to move around, interact, and connect, and we minimized the likelihood that they'd sit holed up in a cube all day not talking to anyone and developing high blood pressure from stress and aloneness. I think everyone at Rackspace felt terrific about renewing a dead space and giving it new life.

Then again, even after spending a hundred million dollars, our building always did and would remind anyone who stepped foot in it of a mall. We started referring to our transformed mall as "The Castle," an ironic take on Windsor Castle, where the British monarchy live. We loved that we now had an open work environment, that our building served as a metaphor for our ambition to be something great, that it spoke to our desire to serve community, and that it physically embodied our culture and desire to ensure conditions under which people could volunteer the best that they had.

You could sense the Rackspace energy from your approach

to the building at the impressive entryway and inside, as well. Our office space became a symbol of our company's culture and our commitment to San Antonio.

In an October 12, 2012 *New York Times* article, journalist Kate Murphy wrote:

> Shops and restaurants now encircle the mall, hoping to lure Rackspace employees, whose average salary is $69,000, far above the local average of $37,000. Stratford Land, a real estate development company based in Dallas, purchased 111 acres nearby in January, promising to build restaurants, shops and multifamily housing for Rackers. . . .
>
> "We feel blessed and fortunate to have the right space at the right time for Rackspace," said Rafael Castillo, Windcrest's city manager. "They've given us a sense of stability and opportunity going forward." Windcrest's tax revenue has increased 10% every year since Rackspace acquired the mall, and the city expects to be debt-free by 2014. With these results, it's hard to find anyone in the city who begrudges Rackspace's generous incentive package.
>
> Perks include free soda machines, an exercise room, coffee bar, recreation areas for playing video games and meals catered daily by different area restaurants. The company also sets up an enormous white tent in the parking lot every Tuesday and Friday, under which 10 to 12 food trucks park, lending a festival atmosphere at lunchtime.

We finally had a space that reflected who we were and helped us recruit people to Rackspace and San Antonio. I think physical space should reflect a company's culture, and our office space emphasized our beliefs in openness and communication. The Castle helped everyone do their jobs better, and the business world noticed. In 2008, the year we moved into The Castle, *Fortune* magazine ranked Rackspace 32nd of the 100 Best US Companies to Work For.

Lifestyle

On a composite cost of living scale, San Francisco is at 177% and San Antonio is at 86%. San Antonio is very affordable, and that's its secret sauce. San Francisco features an average 90-minute commute each way and is one of the top-10 most polluted cities in the US. Plus, although San Antonio doesn't have an ocean, mountains, or a redwood forest, it has the austere Texas Hill Country, an interesting Mexican heritage, the best rodeos you'll ever attend, the San Antonio River, Texas pride, and a small community feel. Plus, it has Fiesta!

The low cost of living makes San Antonio a good place to start a company, I think.

CHAPTER 16

Who We Are

By 2007, we were a team of 2,000 people, energetic and passionate about our work. We had a very low employee turnover rate of 6%, and our undesired turnover, which is departures we didn't want, was even lower.

I loved leading our monthly all-hands, open-book meetings because I believed one way an executive shows respect for employees is by being candid. I despise closed-door meetings, talking about people when they aren't present to defend themselves, and assuming people have negative motives. I invite differences of opinion and respect people even if I disagree with them.

During the internet-bust when our financials stank and we had to lay off people, I had shared our financial information with everyone, and I continued that approach. At our monthly meetings, I outlined financials and progress against goals, and took questions, after which I introduced new Rackers. I remember one introduction of a new Racker who knew karate:

Me: "Okay, so what's your name and what will you be doing here?"

Matthew: "I'm Matthew,* and I'm working in tech support."

Me: "Welcome to Rackspace, Matthew! And what exactly will you be doing in technical support?"

Matthew: "Um, I'm not really sure."

Me: "No worries, I'm sure you'll figure it out soon. Matthew, tell us something about yourself that we don't know."

Matthew: "Well, I'm a black belt in karate."

Me: "That's awesome, dude! Can you give us a demonstration?"

Before I knew it, Matthew had karate chopped the hell out of an office chair. That impressed me. I loved the monthly mini-talent shows because Rackers had amazing talents. Some people broke out wicked hip-hop moves—I remember one Racker spinning around on his head like a top. Others sang, juggled, or rode a unicycle.

I ended our monthly meetings by asking new people whether they wanted to tell a joke or sing a group song. Young guys sometimes chose the joke-telling, and their choice was fine by me, but I felt obliged to give them guidance. "Look, home slice," I explained to the ones who chose joke-telling, "telling a joke is fine as long as you keep it clean and inoffensive."

For everyone else, I usually made up an inane tune to eliminate the discomfort of looking dumb in front of

---

* Matthew is not this guy's real name. I made this up to protect the innocent.

Rackers. We performed our customer service jobs in front of other Rackers, which meant we needed to be comfortable looking uncomfortable. Customer service calls could prove challenging—the ego-equivalent of singing a dumb song with a bad voice.

I once introduced a new account manager, Jason Carter. He had taken a pay cut from a job at a big media company to join Rackspace. He majored in English as an undergraduate, attended film school, and had no technical background. But we thought he had the right mix of willingness to learn, outgoing sales personality, and desire to embrace our culture. I asked him at his first monthly meeting to choose a joke or song.

Jason lit up. "Oh, I want to tell a joke!"

I gave him the warning about keeping it clean, which he heeded, but I could tell from his openness to looking foolish that he understood our culture. On his first day of work, we had him poll our customers, calling clients to ask how things were going. New employees did this because I felt strongly that Rackers had to understand our customers not as abstractions but at a concrete level, as real people who had very busy work days. If our customers were frustrated because they didn't understand something about Rackspace, our associates needed to know.

I made polling calls sometimes, but about half the time, customers didn't believe it was really me.

Customer: "You're the CEO of Rackspace?"

Me: "Yeah, we call customers to ask how we're doing and . . ."

Customer: "Wait, I don't believe you're actually the CEO."

They sometimes said they were going to hang up and call back through the main line to confirm it really was the CEO of Rackspace calling them.

We used Net Promoter Scores, a system trademarked by Bain & Co., that enabled us to accurately measure the approval and loyalty of our customers. With Net Promoter Scores, we asked one question: "On a scale of 1-10, how likely is it that you would recommend Rackspace's products and services to a friend or colleague?" We then classified a customer as a promoter, passive, or detractor. This was probably the most important metric we used to understand the health of our business. It provided us the customer intelligence we needed to quickly see patterns and set priorities.

Jason did his polling calls and ended up doing an awesome job in sales support. On a few occasions, he encountered customers with urgent technical issues and had to suffer through calls that lasted 12 hours, but Jason was an archetypal Racker: He stuck with the customer until the problem was solved.

CHAPTER 17

Roaming Around

I never could figure out which employees would, like Jason Carter, have a long-term horizon and move up the ladder versus which ones would quickly burn out and leave. I found that hiring people was the hardest part of growing Rackspace. We didn't know what we were getting until we had worked with someone for a while and had the opportunity to see how they operated under pressure and during hard times.

One way I tried to stay close to our culture was to walk around our offices and find out how employees were doing, which people call "Management by Walking Around." Thing is, I roamed more than I walked. Ironically, I based my roaming on the ADHD version of a concept that I got from Jeff Gibson at Table Group, a consulting firm. Its advisory services are based on the work of Pat Lencioni, who wrote *The Five Dysfunctions of a Team*, which I loved. The company's name is based on the belief that the most important and effective tool in business is the table. There's no substitute for the idea of people sitting around a table to resolve the critical issues relating to their business.

The idea of connecting to people face to face appealed to me, but because I am restless, I preferred to be on my feet instead of at a table. Every day, I roamed around the Castle—a chubby, bald guy in jeans, cowboy boots, and button-down shirt—and asked questions of employees, listened to them, and talked with them, intent on learning the good, bad, and ugly of our operations. I took the most interest in the problems, which leads to the other marketable skill I think I have (beyond the skill I already mentioned of getting people to do seemingly impossible things): I'm pathologically candid.

A lot of business managers claim to want to hear complaints and bad news, but in practice, these managers react negatively when they hear these things, and they stigmatize the people who deliver them as complainers. That's a natural reaction. Managers are working hard for things to go well, and when associates complain and deliver bad news, managers take it personally. Managers don't do a good job of stepping back, and they blame the messenger.

I invite completely candid feedback to the point that I think I'm genetically wired to prefer candid information to pleasing information. Whether I *want* to hear the news being delivered has always been irrelevant to me. I try to separate my personal feelings from the difficult information and not take it personally. The primary way I practiced this at Rackspace was to wander around, ask for good or bad information, and remember to reward, not shoot, the messenger.

The Castle was a perfect environment for roaming around. The mall layout made the company feel like Main Street. I remember one day when Frederick Mendler, (aka

Suizo), our VP of Support, came running down the hall looking distraught.

"What's up dude? You look like crap," I said.

"Man, I totally screwed up!"

"What's wrong? Is the network down? What's happening?" I asked.

"I sent it," he said.

"You sent what?" I had no idea what he was talking about.

"Lanham, I accidentally emailed the salary spreadsheet to everyone," he said with anguish. As leader of his department, Suizo had access to a spreadsheet that included the salaries and proposed raises for his entire department. He had accidentally sent it to the nearly 90 people in his department.

"Oh, dude! Oh, man! You did screw up! I guess the good news is everyone has complete transparency on where they stand in this company. We'll find out if they agree with their compensation or not because now they have perfect information." Then I took him out to dinner at a Mexican restaurant. I wanted him to know he had done the right thing by quickly telling me about his big mistake.

My method of candid communication through roaming around didn't always come across benevolently. I remember once a Racker came running down the hall to tell me our network was down. This is about the worst thing anyone can hear at a company that has a 100% uptime guarantee. I ran down to an engineer's office, and by the time I got there, the network was back up. I was glad the engineers had told me about the problem immediately, but I pulled the team together for what I called an "autopsy without blame." I wanted to have the conversation with everyone right then in one room. I have an open door style, and I don't pull people behind closed doors for this type of thing. Whether praise or disagreement, I like everything out in the open. This makes work like being on a playing field or a construction site, where everyone gives and receives real-time feedback.

"Timeout. We're all going to talk right now and figure out what happened so it doesn't happen again," I said.

An engineer had entered a fat-finger command, and his carelessness had caused a few minutes of downtime, a window brief enough that customers may not have even have known about it. I said that mistake couldn't happen again, but I didn't punish anyone. My feeling was that at least they had told me about it and diagnosed it.

I roamed around a lot because that kept me closer to the action and focused on people more than on numbers. But roaming around had one effect about which I was ambivalent. In regularly roaming around, I naturally became friendly with Rackers. This was risky business because I ended up occasionally having to fire a Racker with whom I had become good friends. After these infrequent firing occasions, I decided I wouldn't become friendly with Rackers anymore during my daily roam-abouts or at any other time. I decided that making friends with team members wasn't worth the toll it took on me when I had to fire someone. I shouldn't get so involved with people; it compromised my objectivity. I decided I'd be completely professional and cordial but not casually friendly.

But I *never* could stick to that decision. First, that wasn't my personality; second, I'd be going against one of our core values, to treat each other like friends and family; and third, I liked Rackers too much. I wanted Rackers to perform well and felt the only way for me to lead was to stay close to and casual with them. Inevitably, after I recovered from the difficult experience of having to fire someone I liked, I always ended up resorting to my nature and becoming friends with Rackers. I didn't know how to lead or manage any other way.

There's one particular Racker I never became friendly with and whom I didn't mind firing, though. I received a call one day from Karla Fulton in Human Resources.

"Lanham, come on over here, we need you!"

I walked over to her desk to find three US Marshals waiting for me—guns and badges right there, no introduction.

"Have you seen this guy?" one asked. He slid pictures across a table.

"I don't know. Should I have seen him?"

"Yeah, he works for you," the Marshal replied. "He strangled and buried a medical student three years ago in Big Bend National Park."

How the heck could we have hired someone who was wanted for murder? We made sure to conduct background checks before we hired every employee. (I later found out that he committed his crime on federal land. Federal crimes didn't show up on the state background checks we did. We quickly closed that loophole.)

It turned out that he worked the night shift at Rackspace.

The marshals wanted to set up a sting operation in our offices.

"We want to get this guy when he comes into work," Marshal #1 said. "You call him into the office, and we'll arrest him when he walks into the office area."

I wasn't having any of that.

"That's crazy! What if he gets away, takes your weapon, and shoots the place up?" I asked.

"We'll do it in the main lobby of the building then," the marshal suggested. (This was back when Rackspace was on the fifth floor of the Broadway Bank Building).

That's what we settled on. Karla called John (the bad guy) to lure him into the building. Her voice was wavering, which I hadn't heard much before because in every respect, Karla was rock-solid, amazing, and the type of person every company needs. She set up our original human resources function and became the mother hen of Rackspace. She cared deeply about people and served as a wonderful role model for everyone at the company. I loved her to death, and to me, she represented everything positive you would ever want to work with. Most of all I admired how she managed to be strong and caring all at once. She sent my kids birthday cards—she still does to this day—not because it was an HR tactic or anything she'd learned or been told to do to increase engagement, but because she's a caring and personable person. Whenever she organized our Rackspace celebrations, I knew they'd exude warmth.

Hearing Karla's nervous voice on the phone made me even more nervous. "Do you think you can come in to the office? Payday is coming up and something's wrong with your paperwork," Karla said to the murderer. "We need you to sign some forms."

Karla and I stood there with the marshals, waiting for John in the main lobby on the first floor. I felt like James Bond except for the fact that I was chubby, bald, and nervous as hell. John walked in and the marshals moved toward him, showed him their badges, and arrested him. Fortunately, having suspected nothing, John didn't try to shoot up the place, nor did he resist arrest. The federal courts eventually convicted John and sent him to jail, which meant I had officially hired a murderer.

Sometime later, one of our Linux technicians, B-Zam (also known as Bob Zamites), saw a notice in a federal all points bulletin that John had accessed a crawlspace and escaped from a West Texas prison. B-Zam got pretty nervous and sent around an email.

"*He's coming back!*" he wrote.

"*Relax, the last place that he's going to come to is Rackspace,*" I responded.

Fortunately, John turned himself in the next day, and authorities put him in jail again.

While I may not be a world-class developer of people, hiring a murderer was not one of my high points.

CHAPTER 18

Fanatical Support

When David Bryce came up with the term Fanatical Support in 1999, co-founder Richard Yoo didn't fall in love with it. He felt that Rackspace.com should be in the tech sector not the services sector. The category a company is in matters because you design your business around the category in which you compete. Richard shared concerns that offering extreme levels of service support to customers who didn't know very much about their technical systems and never would may not be economically sustainable and risked positioning the company too squarely in the services sphere. My interpretation was that Richard, as a tech guy, wanted the company he had co-founded to compete purely in the tech sphere.

Richard wasn't alone. Some others at Rackspace agreed that the company didn't want the type of customer that demanded more than Rackspace could or should provide. On the other hand, many Rackers fell in love with the idea of Fanatical Support, and I was one of them. It was clear to me early on that Fanatical Support was our future. It caught on quickly with customers and employees and became much more than guaranteed uptime and a money-back-guarantee. It became synonymous with the complete satisfaction of our customers as our sole ambition. Anything less than complete satisfaction was unacceptable. It became our strategy.

In 2001, we began presenting a Fanatical Jacket Award to Rackers who provided outstanding customer service—a straitjacket, with the words "Customer Service Fanatic" stamped on the front in all caps. We then created the Fanatiguy®, the man in the Rackspace logo who supported our customers. Fanatical Support included initially a 99.999% server uptime guarantee, and in 2003, we moved it to 100%. For us, downtime was extremely rare, and one cyber research and analysis firm named us "the most reliable webhost."

We made our Fanatical Support promise to all of our customers: We cannot promise that hardware won't break, that software won't fail, or that we will always be perfect. What we can promise is that if something goes wrong, we will rise to the occasion, take action, and do our best to resolve the issue.

We told our customers that if things went wrong and we couldn't fix them, we'd allow them to terminate their contract. We provided customers with 24/7 direct access to a systems engineer. We trained our employees so well that always providing the highest level of customer service went deep into their DNA. Everyone was enthusiastic about our customers. Satisfaction always came first, and our customers fell in love with Fanatical Support.

As part of Fanatical Support, we took a long-term view on customer satisfaction. We took actions that seemed crazy in the short term but served a long-term purpose. For instance, in 2008 during the Great Recession, we actively reduced customers' bills.

Racker: "Hi, this is Heather from Rackspace. I noticed you're not using nearly as much computing as you contracted for, and we'd like to talk about negotiating that down for you."

Customer (laughing): "What? Is this a joke?"

We voluntarily cut back our customers' contracted payments to us during hard times because we knew those customers would stay with us, grow with us, and tell their friends about us.

Here's another example of the power of Fanatical Support. Before the Great Recession in mid-November 2007, a guy drove a truck into a power transformer on the property of a data center near Dallas. This shut down the power, but our back-up generator immediately kicked in.

Thank God we have back-up generators, I thought.

We had built our onsite diesel generators to operate indefinitely in case of extended power outages.

Outside, emergency crews worked quickly to rescue the truck driver, who was about to go into diabetic coma. Confusion among the emergency services people caused the utility power to go on and off multiple times. As a result, Rackspace's power cycled between utility and generator multiple times.

If you're running a data center, you not only need power, you also *always* need to keep the place cool. Thousands of servers operating in an enclosed space generate an enormous amount of heat. Servers do not like heat! They'll melt down or even catch fire without proper cooling, destroying customer data, which isn't good for the customer's business or ours. Point is, it's incredibly important to keep the temperature of a data center within a consistent zone.

We kept our data centers within this cool zone by way of several coolers—massive machines, each bigger than a school bus, outside the data center. Chillers operate around the clock and cool the water used by the HVAC system in the data center. The thing about chillers, though, is that they take about 30 minutes to cycle up and do their job of cooling. They can't be flipped on and off quickly or arbitrarily.

That morning as our power switched between the utility and our generators, the coolers began to cycle on and off. We could have waited 30 minutes for the power on the coolers to cycle up once. But as the power source continued to switch, the coolers re-started multiple times. They never really got going again. Very soon, the heat in the data center rose. The servers were in danger of overheating. This situation was what we later called in our IPO prospectus "simultaneous system failure."

We were left with one dreaded but necessary option: emergency shutdown of our servers.

With our servers shut down, many of our 29,000 customers couldn't access their data.

So much for a 100% uptime guarantee.

An emergency shutdown of servers is a process in and of itself. Just turning off a server can cause data loss; to avoid this we had an orderly process that would require coordination with each customer.

Customers began calling in droves, but many Rackers had gone home for the day. It was our commitment to Fanatical Support that pulled us through. I didn't ask anyone to come back and help out, but within an hour of the accident, I saw

Rackers streaming back into the building. When I walked around the building at 9 p.m., I saw hundreds of Rackers on the phones with customers. Some people brought their families in with them, ordered pizza, and worked while their children slept on desks and on the floor. Many Rackers toiled all night, taking calls from thousands of customers and helping bring their websites back online.

This was the most incredible, uncalled-for employee engagement I had seen in my professional career!

Later, when we contracted with Gallup for some of our metrics work, the polling organization confirmed that the main competitive advantage a company can possess is its employees' discretionary effort, which is driven by employee engagement. During this simultaneous system failure, our dedicated servers were down for three hours, long enough that Rackers thought we'd never recover. But because of Rackers' valiant customer service efforts, we lost only a few customers. We credited their monthly fees to account for the downtime, and the event became a non-event. Not only did we survive, we thrived.

That's Fanatical Support, the core business principle that enabled Rackspace to achieve fantastic growth for many years.

Engagement

Happy employees are engaged employees, and this leads to happy customers. Happy customers stay with your company, are willing to pay more for products and services, require less sales and marketing, and lead to higher profits and shareholder value. The economics of employee loyalty are powerful! In Silicon Valley, employee loyalty is the lowest of almost anywhere in the world (average employee tenure is one year). Meanwhile, a Gallup poll found that the top four cities with the highest percentage of engaged workers are: San Antonio (38.1%), Oklahoma City (37.6%), Riverside, California (36.8%), and Tulsa (36.3%).[6] One element San Antonio has in its culture is loyalty, and I think that leads to satisfied customers. The loyalty and engagement of Rackers allowed Rackspace to play a long-term game.

In 2007, Rackspace bought the shuttered Windsor Park Mall and converted it into new corporate headquarters. The 1.2-million-square-foot facility became affectionately known as "The Castle." We had fun with its unique design, look, and feel; it also became a competitive advantage to us in terms of attracting tech talent. *(Both photos by Jennifer Whitney/The New York Times/Redux)*

I loved our hands-on, monthly employee meetings. We tried to be an open book, and to have fun, too! *(Both photos courtesy of John Engates.)*

SECURITIES AND EXCHANGE COMMISSION

Washington, D.C. 20549

FORM S-1

REGISTRATION STATEMENt UNDER
THE SECURITIES ACT OF 1933

RACKSPACE.COM, INC.

(Exact name of registrant as specified in its charter)

DELAWARE	**7389**	**75-2864797**
State or other jurisdiction of incorporation or organization	Primary Standard Industrial Classification Code Number	I.R.S. Employer Identification Number

March 15, 2001

VIA EDGAR AND FACSIMILE

Division of Corporate Finance
Securities and Exchange Commission
450 Fifth Street, N.W.
Washington, D.C. 20549

Re: Rackspace.com, Inc.
Request to Withdraw Registration Statement
on Form S-1, as amended.
File No. 333-33414

Ladies and Gentlemen:

Rackspace.com, Inc., a Delaware corporation (the "Company"), hereby requests pursuant to Rule 477 under the Securities Act of 1933, as amended, to withdraw from registration the Registration Statement on Form S-1, including all amendments and exhibits thereto (File No. 333-33414) (the "Registration Statement"), originally filed by the Company with the Securities and Exchange Commission (the "Commission") on March 28, 2000, and thereafter amended. The Registration Statement is being withdrawn because of unfavorable market conditions. The Registration Statement was not declared effective by the Commission and no shares of common stock were sold pursuant to the Registration Statement.

We filed to go public in 2001, but with the bursting of the internet bubble, the window broke for IPOs. We withdrew our IPO and focused exclusively on owning our own destiny through becoming profitable. Project Profit and Project More Profitable became our rallying cries.

15,000,000 Shares

rackspace.
HOSTING

Rackspace Hosting, Inc.

Common Stock

This is an initial public offering of shares of common stock of Rackspace Hosting, Inc. Rackspace Hosting is offering 12,700,000 of the shares to be sold in the offering. The selling stockholders identified in this prospectus are offering an additional 2,300,000 shares. Rackspace Hosting will not receive any of the proceeds from the sale of the shares being sold by the selling stockholders.

Prior to this offering, there has been no public market for the common stock. The initial public offering price per share is $12.50. Application has been approved for listing on the New York Stock Exchange under the symbol "RAX".

See the section entitled "Risk Factors" on page 8 to read about factors you should consider before buying shares of the common stock.

Neither the Securities and Exchange Commission nor any other regulatory body has approved or disapproved of these securities or passed upon the accuracy or adequacy of this prospectus. Any representation to the contrary is a criminal offense.

	PER SHARE	TOTAL
Initial public offering price	$12.50	$187,500,000
Underwriting discount	$0.875	$13,125,000
Proceeds, before expenses, to Rackspace Hosting	$11.625	$147,637,500
Proceeds, before expenses, to the selling stockholders	$11.625	$26,737,500

Rackspace Hosting, Inc.

1-day   Aug 8 4:00pm ET

11.5

11.0

10.5

10

10   11   12   1   2   3

RAX 1-Minute ---   (DELAYED +20-MIN)

In 2008, we tried an IPO technique (Dutch Auction) that was fancier than we could successfully implement. Additionally, that year the economy was heading into the toilet. Many advisors wanted us to cancel our IPO, but I didn't want to cancel—we needed cash, and we got it! If we had canceled, we would not have had the cash to bring the company through the crisis.

In between investor meetings for our pre-IPO road show, I watched portions of *Talladega Nights* (photo shows actor Will Ferrell). It was one funny movie, and watching it helped me through a couple weeks of meetings that were rote and formulaic. *(E. Charbonneau/WireImage for Sony Pictures)*

After the IPO, Graham and I (pictured here) and others flew back to San Antonio. We had a carnival-type celebration at Rackspace.

We enjoyed building our modern, wonderful home on property in San Antonio. Dacia chose architects who made sure the house fit in with the environment, centering on a grove of oak trees. She worked hard as a radiologist, and the fact that we could finally celebrate her (and my) hard work with a house we loved made me very happy. *(Courtesy of Mark Menjivar)*

This is the truck I use at our ranch. I love that thing. It's one of my favorite places to be.

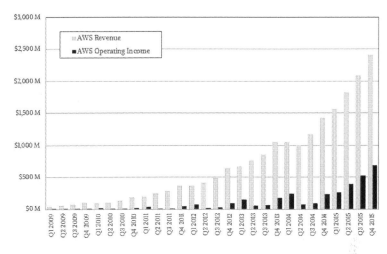

In 2006, when Amazon launched Amazon Web Services (AWS), I saw the writing on the wall for Rackspace. Overnight, we had a competitor with enormous infrastructure and the deepest pockets imaginable. In 2010, Microsoft and Google entered the fray as well. *(Courtesy of The Next Platform, Feb. 1, 2016)*

Data Centre ▸ Cloud

Rackspace breaks billion buck barrier in 2011

Cloudy block storage, database, and firewall in the works

By Timothy Prickett Morgan 13 Feb 2012 at 23:29   1 💬   SHARE ▼

It took twelve years, but Rackspace Hosting has chalked up its first billion-dollar year – and it's hoping to get to $2bn in a lot less time, planning some new cloudy services to help make that happen.

Rackspace hit a billion dollars in revenue in 2011. We threw a party outside The Castle to celebrate. As we entered 2012, I felt happy about our growth. That year, we would reach 4,852 employees, 79,805 servers, nine data centers around the world, and $1.3 billion in revenues. *(Courtesy of The Register)*

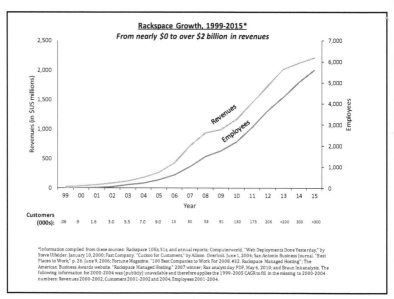

Rackspace Growth, 1999-2015*

From nearly $0 to over $2 billion in revenues

Revenues (in $US millions) / Employees

| Customers (000s): | .06 | .9 | 1.6 | 3.0 | 5.5 | 7.0 | 9.0 | 13 | 30 | 53 | 91 | 130 | 173 | 206 | >200 | 300 | >300 |

*Information compiled from these sources: Rackspace 10Ks, S1s, and annual reports; Computerworld. "Web Deployments Done Yesterday," by Steve Ulfelder. January 10, 2000; Fast Company. "Cuckoo for Customers," by Allison Overholt. June 1, 2004; San Antonio Business Journal. "Best Places to Work," p. 26. June 9, 2006; Fortune Magazine. "100 Best Companies to Work For 2008. #32. Rackspace Managed Hosting"; The American Business Awards website. "Rackspace Managed Hosting." 2007 winner; Rax analyst day PDF, May 6, 2010; and Braun Ink analysis. The following information for 2000-2004 was (publicly) unavailable and therefore applies the 1999-2005 CAGR to fill in the missing to 2000-2004 numbers: Revenues 2000-2002, Customers 2001-2002 and 2004, Employees 2001-2004.

Growing the company to over a billion in revenues and creating sustainable jobs was incredibly satisfying. I'm lucky investors, the board, and Rackers gave me the opportunity to do this. (Also, Dacia gave me the confidence and provided the cash flow to our household to allow me to take a risk on Rackspace.)

PART III

Exit

CHAPTER 19

Our Main Thing

Amazon's entrée into dominating retail began by selling books on Amazon.com in 1994 and then moving into other products. Nearly everyone knows about its steady march toward becoming the largest-ever retail marketplace, consisting of many thousands of companies selling their wares on the Amazon.com platform to many millions of buyers. What some don't know is that Amazon took an even more aggressive approach to its entry into the cloud space in 2006. In building the largest online retail service in the world, Amazon created an enormous infrastructure of servers that supported its business. In 2006, Amazon decided to repurpose this server infrastructure—it created Amazon Web Services, or AWS, and entered the hosting space.

AWS rapidly gained about two hundred thousand web hosting customers. Overnight, we had a competitor with enormous infrastructure and the deepest pockets imaginable. Its entry into our market dramatically raised the stakes and the amount of capital we needed to spend to compete.

By 2008, the capabilities, capacity, and numbers of users of AWS surpassed the capabilities, capacity, and users of Amazon.com. AWS forced us to become laser focused on our strategy. We knew we couldn't outspend Amazon, which was well on its way to the unprecedented market cap that it enjoys today (over $760 billion in Q4 2018).

I knew that although Fanatical Support couldn't be our sole defense, it would nonetheless help us compete. Fanatical Support embodied our total focus on quality in an increasingly commoditized industry and went beyond being an offering—it was an entire system, a philosophy, and a culture. Our combination of strategy, hardware, software, and people had led to the best quality and value in the hosting market. This was the result of constantly working our tails off to offer customers great products and services, and de-commoditizing the hosting business.

I also saw that Fanatical Support had done nothing to deter Goliath-like competitors like Amazon. Somehow we had to figure out how to maintain our quality advantage while growing ever more quickly. Since 2003, we had grown from $59 million in annual revenues and 5,500 customers to $362 million in revenues and 30,000 customers in 2007. That's a 55% compound annual growth rate over four years!

Growth brings tremendous opportunities in the form of jobs, but it also brings threats. I began to study companies that had gone on growth sprees so I could help us avoid their bad examples. Companies like Starbucks, Krispy Kreme, and Groupon had experienced growth pains. On my watch at Rackspace, I didn't want any grow-too-fast messes. I concluded that to compete against AWS, we needed to compete on quality. I would need to manage a challenging combination of very high growth and best-in-class quality.

Every day I went through the front doors at The Castle obsessed with the specific actions we needed to take to maintain the best quality in the managed hosting industry while further increasing our already high growth rate. I remember one time that my difficulty managing this combination struck me. I was meeting with Courtney Pena, who started and ran the Q-Team, the group in charge of lead qualifying for sales.

"Let's mystery shop the Q-Team today," I said.

We needed to be obsessed with providing the highest-quality service to our customer prospects because that's how they became interested in us. Our core, founding concept of the best customer service in the industry should drive our customer acquisition success.

With Courtney sitting next to me, I went to the website and started text-chatting with her team anonymously.

A Racker answered my chat. "Hi, this is Mary at Rackspace. How may I help you?"

"Hello. I'm interested in hosting services," I texted. "Why should I pick Rackspace?"

I don't remember what Mary said, only that some Q-Team members answered right, but many flailed and said the wrong things; there were lots of swings and misses.

Courtney was a stud and handled my experiment extremely well. Listening to these conversations in which we weren't doing our best work to qualify our customer leads was uncomfortable, and she was clearly embarrassed, but she knew I loved her and was testing us as a company, not her.

"Pena, this needs work," I told her.

I was pretty wound up with Amazon entering the industry and the mandate to manage the rapid-growth-and-high quality business model, all without breaking the bank.

"Lanham, I know—I'm sorry," she said.

The industry dynamics causing us problems and my ambivalence about the downsides of very rapid growth weren't her fault. We were in that difficult position of growing too fast and yet not fast enough, and we hadn't finalized our compete-against-AWS strategy. I owed her clearer directives and a budget.

"Okay, let's get to the root of this. We're too focused on ourselves and not focused enough on the customer experience. Each of these experiences needs to lead to a destination and to pull people in. What if you raise this job from entry level and double the pay? What if we call it a Customer Touchpoint job? What technology can we apply here to make a difference? This is about quality of work and not just getting people to go through the motions."

Courtney and I worked together over the next few months on a strategy to enhance the caliber of her team, while continuing to monitor progress via our mystery shopping program. Within months, these efforts paid off and the team was humming—no more swings and misses, but instead, 100% top-quality responses.

Unfortunately, our focus on quality didn't seem to matter as much as I would have liked. The industry numbers showed companies were signing up with Amazon Web Services at an alarming clip. By 2008, AWS had invested over $2 billion in infrastructure and had about 60,000 customers. Worse still, our effort to maintain industry-leading quality and increase our growth rate was taking place precisely when the volatility that preceded the global financial crisis was making companies anxious. Uncertainty was consuming the American business environment. The economy began to slow, and our growth slowed for the first time in years. We weren't shrinking—we never shrank after 2001—but we weren't growing at an ever-increasing rate.

Dacia and I were supposed to take a long-planned, 15-year wedding anniversary trip to Florence, Italy. We wanted to get out of San Antonio for a bit, while our nanny, Jeannie, would take care of Cade and our daughter, Avery (born three years after Cade). We had been planning the trip for two years. But with our growth slowing and my intense unease about increased competition and the need to maintain superb quality, I was wound up too tight to go on vacation. I called her from the office.

"Dacia, I think we've got to cancel our trip," I said.

Because I almost always chose work over family, whereas Dacia balanced both with admirable finesse, this call made Dacia extremely unhappy with me. Marrying Dacia is the single best decision I have ever made, and I could never have joined Rackspace if she hadn't been so amazing in supporting my entrepreneurial dreams. I never could have continued working there without her moral and financial support. But at the time, none of that mattered. I had to cancel our trip. I could see the intense competition in a commoditizing industry coming down the tracks. The company's health—possibly its very existence—relied on me consistently leading our obsession with rapid growth and top quality.

Fortunately, I also had an epiphany about our growth. I had long been thinking of our industry battle as a nearly impossible, two-front war, but it wasn't. I realized that Fanatical Support could fold both those ideas—really great quality *and* high growth—into one unified concept. Fanatical Support was our competitive advantage, and competitive advantages don't hold back growth; they drive it. In business, high quality and high growth don't always make good bedfellows. But Fanatical Support would be our high-growth *and* quality driver.

To communicate this paradox and get people to rally around it and realize we had one unified concept rather than a two-front war pitting quality against growth, I figured I should employ a more mature example than the one I had used years earlier regarding Project Profit—Curly in *City Slickers*, with his middle-finger focus on "one thing." (A little) more mature now, I started using one of Steven Covey's sayings. He said, "The main thing is to keep the main thing the main thing." Fanatical Support—everything it embodied as a quality and a growth driver—would remain our main thing in our fight against AWS.

CHAPTER 20

Sales

To keep growing Rackspace, we had to enhance our sales and marketing capabilities. I had always suffered plenty of bruises when I went on sales calls. I remember once in the early years of Intensive Hosting, we put in a bid to provide exclusive hosting for Spalding, the sporting goods company. Winning the contract would have been huge, not only because of the money but because, as a young company, we needed big, brand-name customers like Spalding. I told our sales team that I'd bring home the contract.

Greg Rodriguez, the Rackspace sales director, joined me on our sales call with the CEO of Spalding. As the discussion unfolded, the tone became tense; I don't recall how or why. Instead of reacting with a soft tone to de-escalate, I reacted with Type-A, aggressive competitiveness.

"I can't believe you're even thinking about staying with [the incumbent vendor]," I said to the CEO. "How'd you even end up with them?"

"I don't really appreciate you saying that about [the incumbent vendor to Spalding]," the Spalding CEO replied angrily. In the next, totally silent moment, I glanced at Greg, and the look on his face confirmed I had officially screwed up the negotiation. The meeting ended immediately.

Back in 2003 when we set our sights on a billion dollars in revenue, I knew we needed to increase our sales success rate, so we had to hire a senior salesperson who had a lot more talent and wisdom than I did. In fact, we had to hire a whole team of people. Gaining additional market share and creating new growth would require hiring a sales leader whose mentality was *one hundred percent all sales all the time*.

We used recruiters and narrowed down the pool to two finalist candidates. Both did what they should have done—they turned the tables and interviewed us. They set up meetings with our sales team so they could assess what needed to be done.

"Your team is terrible," said one candidate.

I appreciated his message, even if I didn't fully agree with it, but the problem was he offered little in the way of potential solutions.

The second candidate was Glenn Ivan Reinus, a man with 20 years of great sales experience. At WebEx, he had been VP of sales and business development, and had built a stellar sales team from the ground up.

"Lanham, you've got a good team. I need a little time, and we'll really get this team performing," he told me.

I agreed with him, and in early 2003, we hired Glenn as vice president of worldwide sales. He had an accurate assessment and offered viable solutions, and I knew he'd be all sales all the time. Glenn had a southern California version of a mullet haircut, which I loved—it was a "business in the front, party in the back" haircut, a truly southern California look.

Right away, Glenn put in place much more scientific measurements than we had previously been using for sales. Within about 90 days of those new measurements, we were hitting our sales goals. He also eventually moved us away from GoldMine CRM and a spreadsheeting system over to Salesforce. We spent a lot of time and money on this implementation, but it was very well worth it.

I did have to figure out how to read Glenn, which took a little bit of time. When Glenn had good news, he ran into the room and blurted out, "Hey boss, guess what?" He launched right into whatever great thing was on his mind. But when something was going wrong, he did the opposite, beating around the bush.

"Boss, how you doin'?" he asked slowly.

"Fine, Glenn. What's up?"

"How's that bad back?" he asked.

"Oh, not too bad, Glenn."

After about eight questions like this, I could see he needed to tell me something, but he couldn't say it.

"Okay, Glenn! What the hell happened?" I asked. Then he spilled the bad news.

Glenn professionalized and systematized our sales, and everyone respected his results even if they did not love his mullet. He quickly became one of the best hires I ever made. But another problem we faced was that we often walked into meetings in which our customer prospects weren't familiar with Rackspace. We needed to improve our marketing— we had cut huge portions of our marketing budget during the dot-com bust and hadn't adequately replaced it over the years.

I signed us up with The Chasm Group for strategic marketing guidance. Technology strategist Geoffrey Moore, who wrote the very insightful *Crossing the Chasm*, founded The Chasm Group. The book title refers to the gulf that separates the innovator and early adopter customers of a technology from the vast majority of customers. Many tech companies can cajole, convince, and persuade innovators and early adopters to buy their products, but then growth stalls because the companies don't have the skills to sell products to the broader marketplace. In the book, Moore offers strategies for moving marketing and sales efforts past the early stages and into the mainstream. Rackspace needed to hit this marketing approach hard if we were going to reach a billion in revenue, so I thought Chasm was well worth the expense.

On a more tactical marketing level, I knew that great companies expressed their thoughts really well, and I wanted us to better showcase our thought leadership through an onslaught of articles, blogs, white papers, and videos. We set out to recruit our own writer, and Graham came across Dan Goodgame. Dan started his career as a journalist at the *Miami Herald* and then reported from the Middle East during the Iraq War. Writing copy that could go up against juggernauts like Amazon, Microsoft, and Google, as we needed to do, wasn't anything close to the Iraq War, but I thought we needed a writer who had mental toughness. After the Gulf War, Dan became the Washington bureau chief of *Time* magazine, published a book, and worked as editor of *Fortune Small Business*.

Dan started as a consultant to Rackspace in 2008, helping

us write our IPO prospectus and other materials, and in 2009, we recruited him to be our VP of executive communications. He wrote well and captured the voice of Rackspace, our people, and our culture, wordsmithing our lingo into copy that helped people make the decision to join as employees or sign up as customers. I relied on him for a lot of my speeches.

Through these sales and marketing efforts and people, we created and held our 50%, year-on-year growth. We knew we were on our way to a billion in revenues. As big as we were becoming, I still loved the fact that San Antonio felt like a small and personable place in which to grow a company. Almost everywhere Rackers went, they ended up seeing other Rackers with their family or friends. When Dacia, the kids, and I were out and about in San Antonio, we usually ran into another Racker and could have a quick conversation, nice laugh, or fun drink. We could introduce our kids and parents to each other. We knew what was going on in other Rackers' lives, and we could express our interest and offer our friendship.

Although we were well on our way to a billion in revenues, I was happy to see the company retain a true sense of community.

CHAPTER 21

Talladega Nights

Starting in spring 2008 as part of the IPO process, I traveled around the country putting on a dog and pony show three to five times per week for a few weeks. Goldman Sachs, our underwriter, organized the meetings with potential investors. The road show started in the smaller financial markets on the West Coast and Midwest, allowing us to hone our pitch before heading to the big-money cities of New York and Boston.

A Goldman salesperson—a different one for every city—accompanied us on each prospective investor meeting. Graham and I started playing a game to see if we could spot the Goldman salesperson as soon as we walked into the lobby of a building, but that turned out to be too easy. The Goldman salespeople were always attractive and well dressed, had "perma-tans," and often looked as if they had just finished working out. We knew them as soon as we entered the lobby.

We had road show meetings in conference rooms on penthouse floors of buildings overlooking whatever city we were in. As each meeting commenced, our Goldman sales-person introduced us. "I'm here with . . . (glancing down at notes to get our names right) Graham Weston and Lanham Napier of Rackspace . . . (looking at the notes some more). "Rackspace is a managed hosting company based on San Antonio, Texas."

It always went that way because most of the salespeople were vapid, and most institutional public equities investors were bozos. I called them C9 investors—portfolio managers for mutual or hedge funds who wanted only the information they needed to fill in cell C9 on their valuation model. I thought they ought to know what they were buying. They were in charge of hundreds of millions of dollars, but they honestly didn't give a flip about what they were buying.

"How are you doing this quarter? What's the number supposed to be this quarter?" someone might ask me.

"Look, dude, we're not allowed to talk about the current quarter!" I typically replied.

The rules of the IPO road show (and of being a public company) are that you can't offer a projection to one analyst but not to the others; you need to give the same guidance to everyone at the same time. No asymmetries in information or preferences are allowed.

"How am I supposed to buy stock if I don't feel good about it?" the investor typically volleyed back with fake naiveté. "This is off the record."

The investor knew he or she wasn't allowed to ask and I wasn't allowed to answer these questions, but sleaze oozed out of these men and women. I once met a big Goldman client who was the founder of a hedge fund. The idea was that he might buy some shares in our IPO. He was a little bitty dude; soaking wet, he couldn't have weighed more than a buck-twenty. He was super smart but all about the money. He showed up in the conference room, and we all sat down.

"Where would you like to begin?" I asked to get the meeting started. "Have you read the prospectus?"

"No," he said.

We've worked for months to put this presentation together, and you couldn't bother to read it? "Would you like us to go through the presentation?" I asked, miffed for the rest of the meeting.

Another time, a young, good-looking guy came to San Antonio and met with us. I could see his suit cost more than my mortgage payment.

"Since managed hosting is a commodity, and we all know Fanatical Support is not real . . ." he began to say.

"Time out," I said and looked at my watch. I didn't like that first line at all, and I needed to let him know. "If you leave right now you can get to the airport and be back in San Francisco tonight," I said. I was totally serious.

He knew he had insulted us, but he didn't take us up on our offer to show him the door; he ended up buying a boatload of stock.

About a week into the IPO roadshow, I realized how to make the meetings much more efficient. I started by asking this question:

"Tell me about your best investment and how long you held it."

If the response was, "I bought X company stock and held it a week," I knew I should leave our meeting early. "You know what? We're not a fit," I learned to say in response.

I wanted us to be built to last, and I wanted investors who

invested in Rackspace for the long haul. I also began combining investor meetings with customer meetings on every trip. This, at least, made the flights worthwhile. And last, I watched *Talladega Nights* between meetings. Many investors weren't trying to pump us for good information; they were trying to pump us for inside information, which they and I knew they couldn't do. Tension builds as you assiduously avoid giving them the illegal information they want. To stay calm and happy in that dynamic, I gave myself seven minutes of *Talladega Nights* in between meetings; I got through our road show that way and enjoyed a great movie, to boot.

Of the two investor types, there were bozos, but fortunately, there also were investors who were brilliant and ethical as they undressed us with their thoughtful questions. The best read our presentation and prepared great questions and insights in advance. Their questions in our meeting went into the weeds around customer adoption, how we did it, and how much it cost. These investors asked about our product offering compared to competitors and about the finer points behind our capital expenditures. They dove deep into our product and customers, comparing pricing by product and customer. They asked pointed but allowable questions to understand what steady-state cash flow generation would look like for Rackspace.

Doug Leone of Sequoia Capital, although a venture capital investor rather than a public markets guy, set the standard for good investors. A partner at Sequoia, he had plenty of investing success, yet he was never cocky. He was so damned smart—he asked piercing questions; came up with a few extremely good, specific ideas; and raised addressable concerns. Doug also introduced me to potential Rackspace customers. He scared the crap out of me, but he energized me, and I trusted him.

The good investors did their homework and pressed us hard, asking us to tell them why we're so great and then holding our feet to the fire. These were people like Henry Ellenboggen at T. Rowe Price, Gavin Baker at Fidelity, and Dennis Puri at Crosslink Capital. I loved Dennis, a Princeton grad who studied computer science and finance. He looked like Rocky Balboa met Albert Einstein. A nerd at heart who loved new technologies and programming, Dennis had dark hair and inquisitive eyes that focused sharply and unnervingly on his "victim" (which was, on occasion, me). He grilled me the first day we met with him, and his questions cut quickly to the core of issues. Not only had he studied Rackspace, but he also knew our competitors.

"Lanham, I don't understand this," he said, staring at me with unsettling intensity. "You said Rackspace was different, but Savvis (one of our competitors) has the same offerings." He went line by line comparing their products, cost structure, and customers to ours. "Why are you so special?"

Wow, this guy is good! I thought. He asked hard, detailed, and good questions. He wanted to know what lay under the surface, and he knew the economics of the industry. I really appreciated his deep knowledge and perceptive questions. When I had to work hard in a meeting, I knew I was in good hands.

"That's the best grilling I've ever had, and if you ever start your own firm, tell me because I'd like to invest in it," I told him. (I would later do exactly that.)

Henry Ellenboggen, the well-known and respected T. Rowe Price investor, had a knack for ferreting out private

companies that were flying under the radar. He sensed potential when others could not. He looked for companies that
offered "a powerful Act I" and were heading toward "a strong
Act II." He was cerebral to the core and a holistic thinker. I
remember hiking with him in Wyoming once during a conference. He had a full head of gray hair, and he listened more
than he talked. But he could talk, too—once he got rolling
on a topic, he always provided a great case study, pulling
information from other industries and applying it to the
case at hand. He did a fantastic job. He had a wide range of
interests, from genetics and biotech to software as a service
and IT infrastructure. We got along well. He liked our team,
Fanatical Support, and how we treated customers, and he
thought we had room to grow, so he bought a big chunk of
the company.

After a few weeks of road show meetings, on August 8,
2008, the day of our IPO, I stood at a podium at the New
York Stock Exchange in Manhattan for the opening bell ceremony. Standing behind me were family members, including my best friend (and wife!), Dacia; my father, and my
brother; and Rackspace executives such as Graham, Glenn,
Lew, Alan Schoenbaum (our general counsel and corporate secretary), Karla Fulton, Bruce Knooihuizen (our CFO
and treasurer), and Jim Bishkin (board member). This time
around, the average age of our executives was 48, compared
to 27 for our aborted IPO eight years earlier. We were a more
mature company in every way.

At 9:29:15 a.m., someone told me to face the cameras.
At 9:29:30 a.m., people on the podium began clapping
(in case the TV networks cut over early to the ceremony);
at 9:29:50, a ten-second countdown commenced; and at

precisely 9:30 a.m., Duncan Niederauer, the CEO of NYSE, needled me in the back as the signal to press the button. I held down a red button for five seconds. The bell clanged, traders and others joined in the cheering, and the market officially opened.

Valued at $1.6 billion with a price per share of $12.50, Rackspace enjoyed a 3.4X revenue multiple, 75X price-earnings multiple, and 6X EBITDA multiple. Those were all derived metrics, however, and what mattered most was that we now had $150 million on our balance sheet. We were listed on the public stock exchange, and any household investor could buy a share of Rackspace. The bureaucratic precision of the pressing of the electronic bell felt totally anti-climactic, and the feeling was underscored by the fact that CNBC had bumped my planned appearance on its news segment. Russia had invaded Georgia that morning, and CNBC thought that was bigger news than the Rackspace IPO.

The group of us flew back to San Antonio on a private jet, and as I stepped off the plane into the 103° heat, I felt dead tired. A couple of golf carts gathered us up, and the Roosevelt High School Rough Rider marching band began playing the school fight song, drums beating and brass blowing. The band led us to a celebration tent on the Rackspace grounds where thousands of Rackers and their families greeted us.

Their cheers were muted, however.

CHAPTER 22

Earnings Reports

The celebration back at Rackspace felt carnival-like, with people eating hot dogs and popcorn and drinking slushies and beer. In many ways, they were happy. We had completed the IPO and raised money. But they had looks of surprise on their faces, like when a kid opens a present that isn't exactly what he or she wanted. People were excited that we completed the IPO, but some had awakened that day thinking they'd be millionaires. They weren't quite as wealthy as they thought they'd be because our public offering price didn't hold up in the IPO. In the first day of trading, the shares closed at $10.00, well below the initial offer price of $12.50.

The good news was that at the Rackspace IPO party, the company felt small and personable. During the road show, Rackspace had started to feel like a collection of numbers because that's all anyone ever asked about. After weeks of traveling and working 90-hour weeks, it was good to be back among friends. But I was dead tired and wanted to take a nap.

I considered our IPO a success. We had raised $150

million immediately prior to the Great Recession, and the money saw us through the financial crisis. Without this cash influx, we would have fared far worse during the recession. Having led projects Profit and More Profitable after the tech bubble burst in 2001, I knew how important it was to get an IPO completed and bring in cash to grow the business.

Wall Street, however, deemed our IPO a failure. Part of the reason had to do with mechanics. We used a modified Dutch auction as our market pricing mechanism because we thought this would be a cool way to do it. A Dutch auction starts with a high asking price that decreases until a participant accepts a minimum acceptable price. We thought we could pull off a modified version of this, but as soon as I saw the Dutch auction playing out, I knew we weren't going to pull it off, and we didn't.

Another reason Wall Street analysts and reporters didn't consider the IPO a success was the asymmetry in what Wall Street valued versus what I valued. Wall Street didn't value the idea of bringing cash in the door immediately the way I did. It became clear in mid-2008 that the economy was going nowhere fast. The Wall Street analysts and reporters weren't running a company, so they had the luxury of theorizing that if we had waited or done something different, we could have brought in more capital at higher share prices later.

Fortune magazine wrote:[7]

> Rackspace took the IPO plunge Friday and fell flat on its face . . . . Trying an initial public offering this year was a gutsy move to begin with. Only four U.S. tech companies (including Rackspace) have tried making their public market debuts in this rocky economic environment,

according to Dealogic . . . . Rackspace, though, had a few things going for it. The company had net revenues of $362 million in 2007, profit of $17.8 million, and steady growth rate, making it the rare tech startup with a track record showing profit growth and financial discipline.

I only wanted to return to running the company as a company, not as numbers and theories. Part of my job involved continual, casual "reporting" to mom-and-pop individual investors. I remember I was grocery shopping once when a city council member came up to me.

"I put a big chunk of my retirement into your company, and I'm taking a bath on it," he said. He proceeded to tell me I stank.

"I feel your pain," I replied, sympathetically. What else could I say?

Much of my job now involved managing institutional investors, which meant preparing for and conducting quarterly earnings calls. The task was simple. We developed a script for the call and attached a page of key metrics. I read verbatim from the script, which was easy. What was trickier was playing a role, like in a soap opera. My role was earning my way into the ranks of credible CEOs. The analysts' role was picking apart my script and presentation. People coached me to make sure that no matter what analysts asked, I knew what I was going to say. With every call, I prepared myself with the three key points I wanted to make, and I repeated them often during the call.

The problem was that I never could help being disarmingly candid, which went against the careful CEO role I was supposed to play. I figured that if I pretended things were rosier than they were by waiting to give bad news or dressing it up as good news, the stock might be strong for a week, but then we'd get hammered on the next call. I wanted to let people know when a situation was bad or when I had no idea how we'd solve a problem so that analysts wouldn't expect magic. I preferred providing and receiving accurate information even if displeasing, and that was a congenital trait.

"You're the only CEO I have ever dealt with who just said 'I screwed up,'" a Fidelity analyst once told me.

One time I screwed up a situation involving Jim Cramer's CNBC show, *Mad Money*, and that bummed me out. After making a boatload of cash as a hedge fund manager, Cramer started his TV show in which he yelled out stock investment advice to viewers in a very ADHD format—lots of props, buzzers, bells, and sound effects. The way he shouted, ranted, and gesticulated, you couldn't quite tell if he was angry or happy about a stock, but he did issue entertaining and informed rapid-fire commentary. I loved his show and thought he was very smart. As an ADHD, bald dude, I felt a kinship with him.

In 2011, he invited me to appear on *Mad Money*, and our PR department thought this would be a great opportunity to talk up Rackspace with investors. We agreed I'd make the appearance. But as the days passed and the show date approached, I became laden with information about Rackspace that I couldn't reveal. The SEC's public company regulations dictated that I could share our information only on a public earnings call. I knew Cramer would do his rapid-fire questioning, and in my rush to answer, I'd mess up what I could and couldn't say, and the SEC would come after Rackspace and me.

I know too much. I'm going to slip up and screw the pooch, I thought.

Two weeks out, on the advice of our lawyers, I cancelled my appearance on *Mad Money*.

Cramer was not happy. He got on the air and publicly railed against Rackspace and me. He later called Rackspace a commodity business that "has lost its mojo."[8] I've always regretted how that went down.

CHAPTER 23

The Rackspace Billion

A billion in enterprise value is considered a bench-mark number by technology standards. People call a company that's financed by venture capital and reaches a billion dollars in value a "unicorn." But I've always preferred a simpler measure—a billion dollars in revenues. Revenues are an enduring measure of value because the top line measures how customers everywhere feel about your products and services. At Rackspace, we were on our way to a billion dollars in revenues, which excited us.

Not all Rackers wanted to join us on our journey, among them, Glenn Reinus, our sales leader. He had joined in 2003 when we were young and needed to create growth in a new market characterized by slow-moving telco competitors. That challenge of creating growth in a new market had really jazzed him. Since then, we had switched our focus from making small sales to small businesses to making large sales to large enterprises, we had moved to a Microsoft platform, we had become a public company, and we had switched from creating a new market to managing our growth in a maturing market characterized by huge, tech-savvy competitors.

These changes had created a situation that didn't much excite Glenn. He wanted to leave. As an offbeat salesman, he was more excited by the younger, more renegade Rackspace than by the post-IPO Rackspace. That had been his career m.o.—he had spent years helping WebEx grow like gangbusters before he left there, too. And so, after five years creating our sales systems and adding hundreds of millions in revenues, he came to my office to meet with me.

"How you doin', Lanham?"

"I'm good, Glenn. What's up?"

"How's your back today?"

"It's doing great, thanks for asking, Glenn. What do you need?"

"Lanham, this has been a real blessing, but I'm not the guy to do this."

I swallowed and tried for a minute to keep a poker face as he explained that he wanted to work at a younger company. But I couldn't poker face this. I took his decision to leave personally, and I told him I didn't want him to go. I loved him, and I thought he was the sales person who would takes us to a billion in revenues. In that meeting and at subsequent meetings, I actually begged him to stay.

I should have come to terms more quickly with the fact that he wasn't directing his decision at me personally. He had enjoyed a successful career, and he knew what stage of growth was the best fit for him. Companies change a lot at each stage of growth, and there's a lot of detritus as a CEO grows a company through those stages, mostly in the form of people leaving.

Everyone has his or her jumping off point on this journey. I deeply wanted Rackspace to reach a billion, and I desperately wanted Glenn to help us. But my wise man with a mullet was stalwart in his desire to leave. He knew himself and his career desires and felt secure in his decision. He made sure his departure never became a personal matter between us. He took time to create a planned, orderly exit from his role as head of sales.

We soon found a new sales leader, Jim Lewandowski, a former prizefighter from Detroit. At about 6 feet 2 inches and 170 pounds, Jim had a great boxing career going for him as a kid until the young Thomas "Hitman" Hearns floored him in a match so badly that Jim walked away and never returned. I personally have Jim to thank for helping me learn about Muhammad Ali, whom I came to appreciate more deeply as the best boxing champ ever and a thoughtful civil rights leader.

Glenn left our team of sales and marketing people the gift of a strong and well structured sales function so that they could meet our billion dollar challenge. They also responded to the bumps we encountered. First, there were the ongoing effects of the Great Recession. Then there was competitive pressure. In 2010, Microsoft and Google entered the public cloud industry. In public cloud, a customer rents a slice of a server or software services from the cloud provider. In private cloud, a single client rents or owns the entire server, making the software and hardware setup less expensive and the financing and accounting much simpler. Amazon, Microsoft, and Google all coming at us in the public cloud officially constituted a tsunami. All were engaged in what analysts called a "race to the bottom" on pricing.

Tactically, we tried to position ourselves in the industry as a differentiated provider of both public and private cloud services. (Managed hosting, our main service since 1999, eventually became known in the industry as "cloud services" or just "the cloud.") Public cloud was harder to execute than private cloud because it required renting out slices of servers to customers who might be on different operating systems and might have different technology infrastructures. The interoperability and interface problems were more complex than in private cloud, where there was a one-server-to-one-customer ratio.

One way we decided to differentiate ourselves and serve customers in public cloud was by co-developing with NASA an open-source platform for public cloud, OpenStack. We knew people felt locked in by the tech set-up they had to use if they signed up for cloud services with AWS, Google, or Microsoft Azure. The AWS, Google, or Microsoft products didn't always interface well with other operating systems and could be pricey. With OpenStack, the code for interfaces and middleware was all open-source code, meaning public cloud customers could access the code easily and free; they wouldn't be locked into paying for the specialized interfaces and connectors that allowed them to access cloud services of Amazon, Google, or Microsoft.

Through OpenStack, we tried to neutralize our disadvantage in public cloud. But even with this public cloud strategy (and our tremendous depth of experience in private cloud), we remained the stand-alone managed cloud company that the huge industry players wanted to roll over. This was the market environment when Rackspace hit a billion dollars in revenues in 2011. We threw a party at the Castle to celebrate.

A billion in revenues was meaningful. It showed that we could do what we had once thought we couldn't do back in 2003 when I had set the goal.

As we entered 2012, I felt happy about our growth. That year, we would reach 4,852 employees, 79,805 servers, nine data centers around the world, and $1.3 billion in revenues. But I also was weighed down with thoughts of difficult decisions we needed to make. They'd be some of the most difficult in our history. OpenStack for public cloud was a tactical maneuver, and a good one, but strategically, we had, as I saw it, three options:

Option One: We could try to go it alone against the behemoths by doubling down on OpenStack as our public cloud option and retaining our private cloud strength. This is what we called a hybrid cloud plan, the main piece being that we would invest in being a public cloud stronghold in the industry through our co-developed OpenStack offering.

Option Two: We could try to get a partner or partners in public cloud, since public cloud required so much investment. That investment from partners would be the capital we simply didn't have access to in the public equity markets. (Also, those partners might end up being acquirers.)

Option Three: We could sell the company either to a strategic acquirer or a private equity fund. With this option, we could "reset" the company and our product suite away from the eyes of the public markets, away from analysts and their quarterly earnings needs. I knew of successful examples of resets, and I thought they needed to be done outside the purview of public markets.

Graham and Lew greatly preferred Option One. (We didn't call these emerging options Options One, Two, and

Three at the time). They saw my favoring Options Two and Three as evidence that I no longer believed in the company. They had already used the words "you just don't believe" once or twice, and they would use them a few more times with me over the upcoming years. They wanted us to stay the course, go with OpenStack—a great product—and believe, as we had always believed, that we could best our competitors.

I didn't agree. I surely "believed," to use their term, but what I believed was that our winning move should be a long-term move. It could take five years to reboot the company to the point where it could be a winner. I believed Rackspace needed a big change if it was going to be "built to last"—it either needed to go private or get a big brother because the change required would involve a five- or seven-year climb. I believed we couldn't make that move in the public markets because they are short term and unforgiving. We would do better to fix our competitive positioning under private ownership.

In the midst of celebrating the achievement of our billion-dollar sales goal, the need to choose and implement one of the three options was weighing me down. I didn't reveal these concerns at home, though. For Dacia's and my entire relationship, I had held the position that I had a completely insecure financial future. I had—exhaustingly, to her—almost never let up on that idea, but now, for our marriage and our happiness, I needed to allow us to celebrate some level of financial security. She didn't care that my insecurities remained the same—that as CEO of a public company with a billion in revenues, I felt just as insecure as when the company was smaller.

I decided it was time for Dacia and me to invest in our

future. After years of hemming and hawing, we decided we'd knock down our house and build our dream home on our three acres. In 2011, Dacia and I met with Tobin Smith from TSA Architects. We told Tobin that we wanted a minimalist home with sleek lines that was integrated with the natural environment. I grilled Tobin for a few hours, loved his passion for what he did, and decided to hire him. We drew up plans to build the new house around a few massive live oak trees in the center of the property, highlighting them.

Billion

Reaching a billion dollars in value is rare enough that venture-backed companies that get there are called "unicorns," a term initially coined by investor Aileen Lee of Cowboy Ventures. According to studies, San Francisco has about 60 unicorns, and Texas has one. San Antonio has none. (Rackspace reached a billion before "unicorn" was coined.) Valuations of companies outside the tech hubs are almost always lower because the ecosystems invest less capital, which suppresses valuations (or maybe robust ecosystems inflate valuations). Whatever the case, I always wanted to celebrate a billion in revenues because it's more meaningful and geographically diverse. I felt you can't argue with the idea of customers around the world paying for products and services to such levels that you're making a billion dollars in recurring revenue.

CHAPTER 24

Offsite

I stopped trying so hard to maintain my strong working relationships with Graham and Lew. First, Graham and I stopped talking on the phone every night. When we were aligned in our strategic thinking, our relationship was straightforward. When we weren't aligned, life in the C-suite became difficult. I had loved our calls for years, and I think we both felt we made each other better through them. When we shared the same vision, we easily added value to each other's thoughts. When we no longer shared that vision, neither of us received value.

I knew my divestment from the relationship was sad and dangerous. A partnership needs to be maintained for its participants to maintain their alignment. When I made the decision to stop working hard on the partnership, I divested from the idea of our partnership as foundational.

With Lew, I was also divesting by deferring decisions about his role. A couple of years prior, Lew, some other Rackers, and I had attended a leadership offsite at a resort outside San Antonio. After the offsite, I was informed that

Lew wanted to resign. I thought: *Damn, Lew is an import-ant leader for us. If I don't keep him, I've failed.* When we met, I decided I'd better do what it took to keep him at the company. In retrospect, a better course of action would have been to let him do what he wanted; when people want to leave, you need to let them go. But Lew was so smart and had contributed so much to Rackspace that I wanted to try to keep him, even if it meant putting up with his dissatisfac-tion with Rackspace and me. I managed to keep him at the company, but by then, we had grown tired of each other, and our "world-class partnership" deserved a major downgrade in status.

As Graham, Lew, and I were quietly growing apart, an enormous company in the industry delivered a gift to us: It asked whether we wanted to partner in public cloud. This was Option Number Two!

Holy shoot, this is awesome, I thought. *Now we can get closer to one of the public cloud players that's gonna make it.*

This very big company could spend its way out of any tech problem. It took me two seconds to decide I really wanted this partnership with BigCo. BigCo wanted to begin the proposed partnership using its legacy architecture and then progress to its new offering in public cloud. Its strat-egy was to use Rackspace as the exclusive provider of the Fanatical Support bundle to its public cloud clients. In the term sheet, BigCo committed to meaningful volume, and it had already invested a lot in its cloud infrastructure. With BigCo as our partner, we'd provide the service capabilities and expertise, and BigCo would provide the infrastructure. We'd be a powerful, public cloud partnership.

Rackspace could then focus on expending capital on

private cloud, where investment in servers and software is much lower. Rackspace could win in private cloud and partner for public cloud dominance. Perfect, except for one problem—Graham and Lew didn't agree with this view at all. They wanted Option One, doubling down on OpenStack as our public cloud offering, which meant not partnering with other companies.

I cannot believe this, I thought. I was torqued.

I told Graham and Lew we needed to do an offsite to air our differences. We went to a conference room at the Hotel Contessa, overlooking San Antonio's Riverwalk, to discuss the BigCo partnership offer. We wrote with markers on large pads of white paper on easels. I argued in favor of Option Two. I didn't think we should invest capital we didn't have into a commoditizing public cloud industry. We should partner. Everyone in the $25-billion cloud infrastructure market knew public cloud had become a cost-driven, commoditized industry. An Oppenheimer & Co. analyst summed up the situation in his Oct. 23, 2013, research report:[9]

> From a technology and platform perspective, Rackspace is clearly in a transition between what has been a successful past (dedicated web hosting) and how it views its future (Cloud IaaS – OpenStack). Positively, it has a strong product niche in being able to sell both public and private cloud, combined with substantial experience in porting companies from client server to the cloud. It also has the best customer care in the industry. This said, the company faces some meaningful challenges in this transition…Perhaps the most significant challenge facing RAX,

at least from the market's perspective, is the pricing pressure applied to the industry by AWS. By our estimates price declines for EC2, the most foundational portion of the AWS cloud, have been around ~12% per year.

BigCo was a dream partner for Option Two. We needed to ride into public cloud on BigCo's back with our hybrid strategy of supporting customers in public cloud and doubling down on private cloud on Rackspace infrastructure.

But Graham and Lew wanted Option One. They felt Rackspace should continue investing in OpenStack as our public cloud offering. Their position infuriated me, but they held firm and united, and I could do nothing to change their minds. We took our disagreement to the board, and its response completely dismayed me. The board believed we should pursue Option One, not Option Two, so we shouldn't pursue the partnership with BigCo. The board believed pursuing Option Two meant getting in bed with the competition, and the board had no interest in that. They wanted OpenStack or bust.

I detested this decision. The mandate to pursue Option One felt to me like being told to bring a knife to a gun fight.

Driveway

The offsite didn't go well, and the board decision didn't go well.

"I feel like a dead man walking," I told Graham and Lew.

They interpreted that as fatigue, but what I meant was that I didn't have the tools to win the fight. Graham and Lew viewed my strategic desire to partner or sell as me giving up on Rackspace. They interpreted my comments and actions as me being tired.

Actually, I was tired. The travel had beat me down a bunch. I missed my family a lot. I was tired of flying everywhere all the time. I was cranky. But mostly, I was tired of not being able to pursue the strategy I believed in.

"You just don't believe, Lanham," they continued to say to me.

"Dudes, I'm just dealing with the data."

It had nothing to do with belief in anything—it had to do with the facts. It had little to do with fatigue, other than that I felt fatigued by battling them over decisions that looked obvious to me. But they thought that I didn't believe in the company anymore.

I think partnerships naturally fray, and the changing industry made it worse. When you're not winning, everything gets exposed. Our partnership was in decline bordering on freefall. On my end, I wasn't going to give up on Option Two. We couldn't rely on OpenStack as our main tactic for winning the infrastructure wars.

Soon enough, I developed another path for Rackspace. Our sales team in London received a call from someone at a European telecom company. The company wanted us to put our code on its hardware, and both the European telecom and Rackspace could offer this as a private cloud option to customers.

This led me to thinking, *If we partnered with a bunch of infrastructure-rich telcos, we wouldn't have to invest our own capital to build out a massive infrastructure to compete with the big guns. We could use the data center and server-rich infrastructure of others.*

I liked this telcos-as-partners strategy. *We should call up CEOs of more telcos and forge a telcos-partnership-plan.*

They'd buy the gear, and we'd put our code into their gear and manage their cloud services. This put Option Two—partnering for public cloud—back on the table, which I loved because there was a zero chance that we could invest enough capital in enough servers to match the capacity of Amazon, Google, or Microsoft. By now, Amazon had a physical infrastructure for its AWS cloud business that you could barely believe. One estimate put the number of servers it had about six years into its existence at 2.8 million to 5.6 million, enough capacity to support a $2.55 trillion e-tailing business.

At Rackspace, we had about 100,000 servers.

On top of the telco hardware, we'd offer our private cloud code and our Fanatical Support. With Jim Curry and our business development team, we generated interest from several telcos, our former competitors; collectively, they had tons of infrastructure. I met with the European telco and another international telco, and both companies loved the idea. Then I received a call from a company owned by one of the richest businessmen in the world telling me his telecom team wanted to run our software and implement our Fanatical Support on its servers. Soon enough, we gained interest from two other companies, one in the US and another one international.

This was awesome. With these partnerships, we'd go from 100,000 servers to 300,000 servers with virtually no capital expenditure. We'd catch up on scale by using other companies' scale. I was extremely pumped about this and had our marketing people create a press release to announce our new telco partnerships.

Then the wheels fell off. The night before we were going to issue the release, Lew called me, enraged. I was at home, having just returned from Cade's baseball game. As Lew spat out his anger, I walked outside to the driveway, where it was hot and getting dark. If Dacia heard us yelling at each other, she'd ask hard questions about work and my relationship with Graham and Lew; I didn't feel like having to explain our disagreements to anyone anymore.

Lew was vehemently against partnering with telcos, maintaining his position that it had to be our infrastructure and our facility. Clearly, he wouldn't reverse his view that Rackspace had to go with OpenStack as our core offering (Option One).

I had to remind myself that I was the CEO. Walking around in the driveway that night listening to Lew's anger, I realized that since I had become CEO I had not managed my relationship with him as president and board member as well as I had planned. Instead, I had for years empowered him to debate with me for too long in areas where he disagreed and then to escalate to the board matters that should have been handled by me. Certainly, he was very capable of handling the president role. It wasn't a capabilities problem; it was a fit problem. Our decision-making styles were too different.

"Look, Lew," I said. "I'm sorry you can't see how being a software company that powers private clouds around the world is more powerful than running public clouds ourselves, but . . ."

With tremendous exasperation, I continued to explain the strategy I had long explained. The approach we needed to take was not a personal slight to him, I explained.

"Lew, I'm doing very simple math," I said. "Here's the math. We don't have $5 billion in capital expenditures."

That's what Amazon alone spent, never mind Microsoft and Google.

By this point, Lew and I were really angry with each other. No matter what argument I presented or how fiercely I stated my case, he voiced his opposition with equal or greater conviction. I finally said I'd delay the press release until we could talk it through with the board.

And what do you know? The board did not approve the telco press release. They had always told me I needed to get Graham on board with me for them to vote yes on big decisions. On the telecom companies matter, Graham agreed with Lew. In fact, their partnership with each other was strong because they both wanted Option One and because I had basically divested from my partnership with them.

Without Graham on board with Option Two, my approach wouldn't be approved. The board reiterated its consensus view that at Rackspace, we would pursue Option One, offering our customers only our own server infrastructure and only in our own facilities.

In their demurral of my plan, Graham, Lew, and the board members never used the words "David and Goliath," but I felt this was the vision they had. I felt they wanted to believe in the power of the little company against the big company. In the biblical tale, Goliath wore armor and stood 6 feet 9 inches tall. Meanwhile, David was a short teenager with a slingshot. David beat Goliath through superior strategy and use of his weapon.

I love the lesson of David versus Goliath. I believe in the power of David, too. I had believed in the power of David since I had joined Rackspace, back when the telcos were the Goliaths. But now things were different. In the Bible, David beats Goliath *because he has superior strategy and use of his weapon.* By requiring that I pursue Option One only, Graham, Lew, and the board weren't giving me superior strategies or weapons. I had no winning strategy. I didn't think becoming more upbeat, open-minded, and creative in pursuit of Option One was going to work for Rackspace or me.

I decided I would not slug it out with Goliath if I had no weapons for the battle.

CHAPTER 26

David

Industry participants didn't talk specifically about David and Goliath, but the industry buzz was overwhelmingly centered on the general idea of the smaller player beating the huge one. Here's a post written by cybersecurity company Upguard:

> Microsoft's Azure and Rackspace Cloud are two competitors in the hotly contested cloud computing market. Other large players are Amazon's AWS and Google's Compute Engine.
>
> The colossus in this market is of course Amazon. Its dominant shadow looms large over the whole cloud computing marketspace, so it's no surprise that competitors are forced into specialization and differentiation of their offerings so they can compete with Amazon's low, low prices and massive resources. Rackspace tries to differentiate itself by its excellent support and customer service, dubbed 'Fanatical Support', in addition to hosting every-

thing on OpenStack—the open source hosting and technology stack.[10]

Industry participants and analysts (and we at Rackspace) agreed that Rackspace would have to compete in the market on its history of sterling customer service, flexible middleware, and many service options. The industry storyline was that Amazon would gain cost advantages through unprecedented economies of scale, and accelerate and grow. Analysts positioned the quality of Fanatical Support against the quantity of the low-cost providers. The industry structure revolved around pitting the sizeable beasts against Rackspace, the nimble company with experience and service. Industry participants anxiously observed David facing the ever-larger Goliath.

Paul Ausick, senior writer for *24/7 Wall Street*, wrote in August 2016 about our evolving market position, "What we're likely seeing here is a race to the bottom on pricing. Being in such a race with the likes of Amazon, with its focus on growth as opposed to profits, or Apple, with the deepest pockets in the known universe, is a near-guaranteed loser."[11] And John Furrier, a Palo Alto entrepreneur, blogged about our industry's price competition in *Medium* in January 2015:[12] "Amazon's AWS price cuts are as frequent as a politician's photo opps, having dropped prices forty-two times between 2008 and March of 2014."

In the deteriorating environment, Lew, Graham, and I absolutely couldn't agree on the path we should take. I realize now, but I didn't then, that partnerships fray, markets change, business is dynamic the seeds of destruction are always there, and everything is temporary. Yesterday's juggernauts aren't today's juggernauts, and today's juggernauts won't be the juggernauts of tomorrow. Everything's moving; there is constant flow. Success isn't a natural state. The natural state is, I believe, for companies to fail.

As far as power goes, I think Graham and I would point to each other if asked, "Who had more power at Rackspace?" Graham had more stock and was chairman, but Graham thought that I set the board agenda and board members supported me more. Indeed, the board had for years generally approved what I wanted Rackspace to do but always with this caveat: I first had to make sure Graham approved.

I had decided I would not pursue Option One because that option had me playing David versus Goliath. Instead, I brought in two top tech-industry consulting firms to see if they could convince Graham, Lew, or the board to pursue one of the other two paths. People told me that in meetings with the consultants, near-screaming fights were breaking out. Lew didn't like the consultants' take on the market at all. As a highly data-driven guy, he didn't think their analysis or conclusions were right.

I began to pursue Option Three on my own—selling or going private—so we could reset our strategy under a new owner. We'd take time to come up with a whole new product offering in an adjacent category, as Apple had in music and we had with Fanatical Support and Intensive Hosting. We needed to operate in private, where our built-to-last philosophy could thrive. Also, a private owner would resolve the frayed partnership among Graham, Lew, and me however the owner wanted to resolve it. I wanted us to do this reset, to operate under our built-to-last philosophy, and to resolve our profound disagreements outside the public markets.

Amazon

The size and scale of Amazon Web Services is staggering. By the fourth quarter of 2018, it had a market cap of around $760 billion. Only Apple, Alphabet (aka Google), and Microsoft are larger. Amazon sales account for 15% of all online sales, and if you count Amazon Marketplace, the number rises to 20 or 25%. Amazon Web Services is the mother of all cloud computing, with more than a million companies relying on the AWS infrastructure, and its cloud service revenues dwarf those of Microsoft, Google and IBM *combined*. Some estimates have put Amazon at having more than two million servers globally. When you're facing AWS, you're facing a mighty foe.

CHAPTER 27

Option Four

I explained to the board that our only remaining option was to pursue Option Three—selling or going private. They didn't strongly disagree, so I went out to generate expressions of interest. I wanted us to attract offers from big industry players also trying to arrive at ways to compete against the behemoths.

I received a call from the CEO of a huge, brand-name company. This bigwig was part of the "tech mafia," the term I used for the CEOs of huge tech companies. "Lanham," he told me, "I want to see if we can be friends. I don't mean the enemy of my enemy as my friend. I mean *real friends.*"

I loved that line, I thought as soon as he said it. *I gotta figure out how to use that, one day.*

I generated interest from other firms, too. I wanted to entertain the offers in an organized manner. In July 2013, with it hot as hell outside, I went into a routine board meeting at the San Antonio Country Club, which was frigid cold. I told the board about the expressions of interest, and the directors instructed me to start the conversation with the tech-mafia CEO and the other companies.

Thank you, Lord!

Although I was happy with our plan, Lew seemed very unhappy. Most important, he was deeply needed at home because his wife had been diagnosed with cancer. He wrote about it in Rackspace's public blog: "Given these circumstances, I have taken some time to assess my ability to balance the demands of leading the Rack with the needs of my family . . . I am not leaving Rackspace. I will remain involved as a member of our board of directors, as a committed shareholder, and as a part-time employee advising the company, primarily on strategy and product direction."[13]

He was drained by the disagreements with Graham and me, and his wife was sick. Life unfolds in crazy and unpredictable ways. For all of us, our family is or should be our most important source of strength in good and bad times—especially bad times. Lew needed to be there for his wife's terrible health challenge. I respected his decision to step back from his full-time role, and I knew I'd be pursuing Option Three alone. Before I called back the companies interested in acquiring Rackspace, I wanted advice on how to sell for top dollar. I knew we needed to create a competitive market among buyers, and we'd do that by running a process.

Enter the investment bankers. As much as I disliked investment bankers as a class, I freely admit they're extremely good at creating a market for a company's securities. They can create a frenzy that increases prices.

I turned to George Boutros. At his boutique M&A advisory firm, Qatalyst Partners, George had earned a reputation for being aggressive and negotiating plum deals for his clients. He advised Pixar on its $7.4-billion sale to Disney in 2006, Google on its acquisition of YouTube for $1.7B in the same year, and Sun Microsystems on its sale to Oracle for $7.1B in 2010. He had worked on 500 transactions. His boss once said that George is to M&A what Tiger Woods is to golf.

But George had a tough style to deal with. *Wired* writer Adam Lashinsky said George "intimidates adversaries by yelling at and belittling them." A *Bloomberg* writer quoted an industry executive who described George as evil and said that he was privately known for his "abrasiveness in negotiations."[14]

George got results, however, so I asked him to come to our next board meeting and provide his thoughts. I figured if the board liked his ideas, we'd hire him. George did his due diligence on Rackspace and offered ideas for when and how to sell the company. Unfortunately, Graham didn't like George's views, his style, or both—I don't know exactly. But I do know Graham decided he didn't want us to contract with George. This made me about as angry as I get.

Soon after, I was at a meeting in San Francisco when Graham called to tell me he was headed to Boston to meet with the tech mafia CEO. He was going to shut down conversations with the company.

Holy sh*&! What???

Graham and I were supposed to agree on any course of action, per the board's orders. But instead, he had decided to run his own process for selling the company. Then I found out that Lew was trying to complete a sale transaction with a different public company in the cloud market (call it PubCo). Lew had agreed to advise Rackspace part time, but I felt working to get Rackspace sold went beyond just advising.

The decision against using George Boutros, the phone call from Graham en route to Boston, and the actions by Lew blew me away. We officially had parallel regimes. The advice I would give myself now about the situation is, "You're the CEO; make the hard decision. You need to find a way to move them out of the company before you can sell the company."

At the time, it didn't occur to me to try to do that.

I should have said to Graham and Lew, "This path of working strategically to sell the company is what I'm ready to put everything into, and if you don't support it then I'll do everything I need to do to remove you from the company."

Of course, I would have had to firmly convince the board I was ready to do that. But, if I had put all my effort into terminating Graham and Lew so I could focus on selling the company the way I thought it should be done, I think I might have succeeded. This wasn't so much about who was right or wrong as it was about who would lead us into our next era.

Instead, I became completely caught up in our fraying partnership. I should have said, "The first principle isn't the partnership. The first principle is, do we build or sell? And people have to follow that decision."

What I should have realized is that although who you get on the bus is important in business (to use Jim Collins' term), who you escort off the bus is equally important. If we were going to build the company through Option One, then we probably had the right people. If we were going to sell through Option Three, then I had a lot of people-related work to do. I think if I had done that work, I would have ended up happier.

After Graham's phone call, I sent Jim Curry, our senior vice president and general manager, with Lew to try to make progress in the PubCo transaction discussions. Through all my anger, I was willing to do everything it took to pursue Option Three, but I was skeptical of the likelihood of success, considering we were following no process and using no investment banker.

I was incredibly pissed off. I had no decision-making power. I had responsibility but not authority, and that had been the case for too long. I suddenly became obsessed with my family's financial security and the fact that I had tied up almost 100% of Dacia's and my net worth in Rackspace stock. I called a few coaches and counselors for help with my situation. I felt pretty alone as I tried to work my way through this period of powerlessness, dissension, and unrelenting competition.

I've been pretty dumb to hold all of my stock this whole time, I thought. *I need to fix that situation.*

For years, a banker at US Trust had called me regularly to pressure me to sell small chunks of my Rackspace stock. Financial advisors tell CEOs of public companies to set up their 10b5-1 plans, the mechanism by which executives sell their company stock without concern about selling while in possession of inside information. Insider trading is, of course, a big no-no. In a 10b5-1, an executive sells pre-defined quantities of stock at pre-determined intervals. You can't easily change the plan because the whole point is to create personal liquidity on a foreseeable, consistent basis that is clearly not based on specific information.

When executives who aren't CEOs sell loads of shares into the market, there's little market impact. But the market cares when the CEO sells. So how does a CEO create a plan that doesn't spook the markets? Every time the US Trust banker had called since our 2008 IPO, I had declined her requests to sell stock through a 10b5-1. But when she called in late 2013, I decided to set up a plan to sell a bunch of stock in order to make up for all the years when I hadn't sold.

I didn't think the market would care much about my sale. When Jeff Bezos, who is inarguably important to Amazon, sold stock, the market didn't care. *Hell, I'm a lot less important than Bezos.*

I filed a 10b5-1 plan with the SEC to prepare to sell the stock, with the first transaction to take place in a few months. Then I returned to my Rackspace frustrations, which remained steady and consistent. The PubCo transaction that Graham and Lew were trying to complete on their own fell apart. At the next board meeting, I told the board with deep frustration that because we hadn't used a process for selling the company, Pubco had shut down our potential transaction.

"I'm done with disagreeing on strategy and tactics," I said. "We should organize an orderly transition, and I should leave the company." I suggested a date when I thought I should be out.

Board members stated firmly that the company needed me to stay.

I had no interest in staying. I had been fighting for too long and wanted to leave. Against my better instincts and judgment, I agreed to the board's request that I stay indefinitely. Shortly after the board meeting, my scheduled 10b5-1 plan kicked in, and about 10% of my Rackspace stock was sold into the markets.

I was dead wrong in my assumption that Wall Street wouldn't care about my stock sale. The market reacted negatively to the timing and amount of my 10b5-1 sale, which pissed off the board beyond repair. Their view was that I had just agreed to stay for the good of the company and then sent a negative message to the market by selling my stock. They did not appreciate the paradox.

The day after the sale, we negotiated an agreement for my immediate departure. We agreed I'd use the word "retired" in the press release about my departure. What mattered to me much more than what word was used in the headline about my departure was that for 13 years I had put my heart and soul into Rackspace, and the idea of creating jobs had motivated me. Going back further still, since 1986 when I had seen families uprooted because of lost jobs and lost livelihoods during the Houston oil bust, I had decided I'd be a job creator. I had seen my father lose his clients, and I had lived in fear of not having a job myself. I had to create jobs, and I had to have a job. As I had pursued these goals, my identity had become that of CEO of Rackspace. That was my core, who I was, how I was known to others and myself.

No matter what the market thought about a sale of securities or the word used in a press release, I knew I no longer had a job. On a chilly February day in 2014, I walked down a stairwell of the Castle and ran into Jason Carter, the Racker who had told a joke on his first day at Rackspace and who had subsequently done a great job in sales. When we got together months after my departure, he told me he had never seen me leave the office at 5 p.m. and had wondered what the heck was going on.

I didn't say anything to him. I left the building and never again walked back in. The press release stated, "[Mr. Napier] plans to invest in and advise other entrepreneurial companies following a decision to step away from public company executive leadership. He will remain a consultant to Rackspace for the next several months to ensure a smooth transition."

That night, I realized that there were more than three options. There was Option Four: leave Rackspace. At home, I entered a Lanham Land that was the polar opposite of magical. I had sold my stock and received departure terms that generated a handsome sum of money, an amount that made me very wealthy. But with my identity as CEO and job creator gone, my new wealth didn't matter. For weeks, I curled up in a fetal position at home, unable to see how I could go on, or to sleep or eat.

This was Option Four—me without a job, having lost the sum total of the partnership and strategic battles that had been taking place since about 2012. I felt my life was gone. For many years, I had believed in industry domination by Rackspace. I had been on top of the world. Now, without Rackspace and the business partnership that had sustained me, I could see only a future of poverty and terminal unemployment for my family and me. Shock and depression took over—Lanham Land gone wrong. A clearheaded person would have known that poverty was extremely unlikely, as was terminal unemployment.

I began to see my psychologist, Madeline, every day to work out how I felt, how I should feel, and what I ought to do about it. Knowing I was wealthy and that Dacia loved me unconditionally weren't what helped me return to sound mental health; the simple logic that Madeline presented did. Her disarmingly straightforward reasoning helped me see that the scenario of poverty and terminal unemployment was improbable. She helped me see that everything—including being CEO of a company—is temporary. The median tenure for the CEO of a company listed on the S&P 500 index is six years.

Although I recovered from the intense anxiety, I nonetheless felt broken for about six months.

Spawning

"Spawning" occurs when employees leave an existing firm and start a new firm. Entrepreneurs grow a company until it goes public or is acquired, and then, with their new knowledge and wealth, leave the company to start a new company. There are many spawning examples in software, internet, social media, and biotech. Among the best examples is Google, which spawned Foursquare, Pinterest, and Twitter. Spawning is kind-of the opposite of loyalty because you have to leave a company to be a spawner. Nonetheless, spawners contribute to a more entrepreneurial ecosystem.

CHAPTER 28

Jobs

God put us on the planet for a purpose. My wife's purpose is to be a healer; she saves lives. I admire that. My purpose as a business person is to build a company and create jobs. I desperately wanted to do that in Texas. At Rackspace, we grew in a simple and straightforward way. We created more than 3,600 tech-related jobs in San Antonio and 5,700 worldwide. I'm proud of that simple story. We competed well in our industry, and I'm proud of that, too. When Amazon came down the pike, followed shortly by Microsoft and Google, we had to recalibrate how we did business.

The partnership among Graham, Lew, and me was wonderful for about ten years, static for a couple years, and then crummy after that. For me, the biggest lesson about how I handled our partnership is that there are many possible right paths, but at some point, someone needs to be the decider and decide. An equally important lesson is, to be great, relationships must be cherished and maintained. I stopped doing this with both Graham and Lew. Our partnership was taking too much time during a period when our company needed to move fast.

I regret letting too much space into our partnership relations and doing nothing to repair that problem. But I love what we accomplished together. With thousands of other Rackers, we created and enjoyed quite a ride in a big, important industry. Today, Lew runs a venture fund in San Antonio that invests in early stage software companies. Graham continues to invest in real estate. He also started Geekdom, an incubator in San Antonio, and Lew worked on that with him. They're committed to growing tech jobs in San Antonio. I co-founded BuildGroup, a fund that provides permanent capital so that determined companies can build for the long haul. Our driving belief is that venture capital works for some but not for all, and that sometimes five years (the standard time frame for venture capital investments) isn't long enough to change the world.

Postscript

After I left Rackspace, the company ultimately pursued Option Two, striking partnering deals with Amazon and Microsoft (July 2015 and October 2015, respectively). In 2016, a private equity fund, Apollo Global Management, acquired Rackspace and took it private. This was Option 3, and it was fantastic for Rackspace. Apollo developed a sharp strategy for the company, sold or shut down a couple lines of business, and improved the cost structure, which increased profit margins. It also continued with the Option Two strategy of Rackspace being a partner in both public and private cloud. Under Apollo ownership, Rackspace added Google as a partner. Today, Rackspace seems to be doing the right things. It provides Fanatical Support for customers on top of Google cloud, as well as for customers of Amazon Web Services and Microsoft Azure.

I hope Apollo keeps Rackspace in San Antonio, and I hope that over time, Rackspace spawns entrepreneurs and innovators who create additional new jobs in San Antonio. Our angel investors came from San Antonio. They knew almost nothing about our industry and not much about growing a tech company, but they helped us have a sense of place and enabled us to stay in San Antonio. I think if

Rackspace had started in or relocated to Silicon Valley, the un-techie notion of offering Fanatical Support may have been silenced quickly or died soon after being introduced. I think in Silicon Valley, the notion of adding more software features and investing massive sums of money in expanding server capacity would have been the main mode of growth. At Rackspace, we stuck with Fanatical Support as our differentiator for a long time, and fortunately, Fanatical Support remains a core feature and differentiator at Rackspace today.

It's impossible to say whether Fanatical Support in San Antonio was the single-most right path to take, in terms of settling on it as our growth driver. I believe it was the single-most right path to take to build a company that could, would, did, and hopefully, will, employ a lot of awesome people in San Antonio.

Notes

1. Quote comes from "Growth Is a Commodity," by John Browning and Spencer Reiss in *Wired* magazine, Jan. 1, 2000.

2. Brief description of Joel Kocher comes from "Dell's Kocher Takes Tactics to Artisoft," by Dana Blankenhorn in *Ad Age*, Sept. 26, 1994.

3. Thomas P. O'Neill, Tip O'Neill's son, wrote this in an opinion piece, "Frenemies: A Love Story," in the *New York Times*, Oct. 5, 2012.

4. The first Clinton quote is from an interview with Fox News commentator Bill O'Reilly, Dec. 20, 2011. The second Clinton quote was during an interview on NBC's *Today* show, also on Dec. 20, 2011.

5. Quote comes from "Revitalizing a Dead Mall (Don't Expect Shoppers)," by Kate Murphy in *The New York Times*, Oct. 30, 2012 © 2012 The New York Times. All rights reserved. Used by permission and protected by the Copyright Laws of the United States. The printing, copying, redistribution, or retransmission of this Content without express written permission is prohibited.

6. Gallup figures come from "San Antonio-New Braunfels Leads U.S. in Employee Engagement," a Sept. 10, 2015 press release. Amy Adkins and Sangeeta Agrawal of Gallup are the authors of the underlying report.

7. Quote comes from "Rackspace IPO tanks," by Jon Fortt, in *Fortune*, Aug. 8, 2008.

8. Jim Cramer quote comes from "Cramer: Beware This Dangerous Stock," by Lee Brodie on *CNBC.com*, June, 13, 2013.

9. Oppenheimer quote comes from research report "Understanding the Cloud Chasm," by Oppenheimer analyst Timothy Horan, Oct. 23, 2013.

10. The quote from Upguard comes from "Azure vs Rackspace," a blog post written May 2, 2017 by UpGuard; note that it is after the time period covered in the chapter.

11. Quote is from blog post, "Did Rackspace Shareholders Get Enough From the Apollo Buyout?" by Paul Ausick, senior writer for *24/7 Wall Street*, Aug. 26, 2016.

12. Quote comes from blog item "Exclusive: The Story of AWS and Andy Jassy's Trillion Dollar Baby," by John Furrier in *Medium*, Jan. 29, 2015.

13. Lew Moorman's July 25, 2013, blog post about going part-time, "My New Role," can be found at https://blog.rackspace.com/my-new-role.

14. First quote comes from blog entry "Shut Up and Deal," by Adam Lashinsky in *Wired*, March 1, 2001. Second quote comes from "George Boutros, Tech's M&A rainmaker couldn't care less that rivals badmouth him," by Alex Sherman in *The Economic Times*, Aug. 17, 2016.

Made in the USA
Las Vegas, NV
02 September 2021

29327617R00101